The Righteous Judge

A Study of
the Biblical Doctrine of
Everlasting Punishment

Harold E. Guillebaud, M.A.
(Archdeacon in Ruanda)

ISBN: 978-1-78364-637-1

www.obt.org.uk

****

The Open Bible Trust
Fordland Mount, Upper Basildon,
Reading, RG8 8LU, UK.

****

www.obt.org.uk

The Righteous Judge

A Study of the Biblical Doctrine of Everlasting Punishment

Contents

About the author

Harold Ernest Guillebaud
(1888-1941)

The author was educated at Marlborough and Pembroke College, Cambridge and ordained in 1916.

Despite poor health the call to the C.M.S. Mission Field took him to Ruanda, in 1925, for the work of Bible translation; and by 1932 he had translated the New Testament, the Psalms and other portions of the Old Testament, the *Pilgrim's Progress* and the *Book of Common Prayer*; he had also written a Grammar.

Returning to England in 1932, he served as Curate at St. Paul's, Cambridge, until 1936 when he went back to Africa for one year to translate the Pentateuch and make a beginning on the New Testament for Urundi.

Subsequently the Inter-Varsity Fellowship published his books, *Why the Cross* (1936) and *Some Moral Difficulties of the Bible* (1941), out of which arose the questions dealt with in *The Righteous Judge*, the manuscript of which he only completed at the time of his last journey to Africa as Archdeacon of Ruanda-Urundi, in 1940.

This book was written not long before its author's death in 1941, but not published until 1964. Therefore it contains no reference to any more recent theological writings on this subject.

Foreword

I feel greatly priviledged in being asked to write a foreword to this book of my late friend, Harold Guillebaud. The origin of the book lies in his being invited by the Inter-Varsity Fellowship to write a book on the moral difficulties found in Scripture. The last chapter was to deal with the question of everlasting torment. When he came to this chapter, he found that he could not answer the question satisfactorily himself. The chapter was, therefore, omitted from the book. He then set himself to study the subject, and the result was that the last chapter was expanded into the present book and the question answered in a different way from what he had first expected.

If more preachers and ministers today were convinced of the Scriptural truth of the doctrine which Archdeacon Guillebaud advocates, they would perhaps feel better able to preach more openly and more often the great truths of God's judgment, which are so much neglected today, though so many drift to hell because they lack knowledge of them. Archdeacon Guillebaud's book will not convince every reader, though it cannot fail to interest each one deeply.

Basil F.C. Atkinson,
Cambridge.
30th September, 1964

Preliminary Note

The following definitions of terms apply throughout the chapters which follow.

"ETERNAL PUNISHMENT" is a Biblical term (Matthew 25:46 R.V.) the meaning of which we shall be attempting to elucidate.

The term "Everlasting Punishment" will not be used in these chapters, but "EVERLASTING TORMENT" will be the term used to indicate that interpretation of Eternal Punishment which represents it as an everlasting existence in conscious suffering. This use of terms has not been decided on for the purpose of indirectly attacking the doctrine in question but because "Everlasting Punishment" is the term used in the Authorised Version of Matthew 25:46, and therefore it cannot be used as a synonym for everlasting torment without danger of misunderstanding and confusion.

"PENAL SUFFERING" is the term used for suffering as a part of Eternal Punishment, without any connotation as to its duration.

Introduction

A few generations ago the majority of Christian people were still teaching their children to believe in heaven and hell. Even those who ignored or rejected Christianity had usually some idea of the general outlines of the Christian doctrine of the hereafter. Today, however, the traditional doctrine of everlasting punishment – that of conscious everlasting torment in the fires of hell – because of its intolerable nature, has been rejected by a large proportion of those within the Christian churches, while of those who still believe it, on the grounds that, however terrible, it is the Bible doctrine, many are finding it a burden on faith and conscience which is more and more hard to bear. Who has imposed this burden, God or man, the Bible or tradition? This is a question which needs to examined from the standpoint of wholehearted loyalty to the Bible as the inspired Word of God.

The general silence of the pulpit on the subject of future punishment, together with an unbalanced emphasis on the Love of God, must be reckoned among the causes of the general apathy towards religion of the present day. In so far as men think about God at all, they tend to take for granted that He is so kind and loving that He could not be very hard on any of His creatures, and that all they need to do is to satisfy more or less their own standards of decent conduct, and then they can feel quite easy about the hereafter. It is acknowledged by many who do not accept the Bible teaching on the subject that this is a very disastrous state of affairs, and that there is urgent need of doctrine of future punishment which men can believe and preach.

It would, however, be most foolish merely to search for a doctrine which will commend itself to the minds of men, regardless of whether it is the message of God in His Word or not. Just as in wartime "wishful thinking" about the military or economic situation is both foolish and dangerous, so (but in a far higher degree) is the acceptance of a man-made doctrine about eternal judgment, which is based upon what appeals to human minds, rather than on what God has revealed. If God has not given us any revelation on this subject, then it is really very little use discussing it, for we have no means of arriving at reliable conclusions. The Bible, however, has a good deal to say about it, which purports to be God's revelation, and this book is written in the firm conviction that any valid doctrine of future punishment must rest upon the Word of God at every point.

It is proposed, therefore in the chapters which follow to examine the Bible teaching on future punishment, seeking honestly to discover what the words of Scripture really mean, regardless of whether the results are easy or difficult to accept. This does not mean of course that difficulties will be ignored: we shall attempt the discuss them in their place, in Part 2 of this book. But intellectual difficulties, however grave, ought not to be allowed to influence the determination of what the Bible words mean. The only factor, extraneous to a particular passage, which can rightly be allowed to influence the interpretation of that passage, is the general sense of Scripture itself.

The Righteous Judge

Part 1

Chapter 1: Is Every Soul Immortal?

It is very widely taken for granted that the immortality of every soul is a cardinal Christian doctrine, and this not in the sense that every soul survives bodily death (which the present writer agrees is definitely taught in Scripture), but in the sense that no soul can ever to *all eternity* cease to exist. This belief has very naturally influenced the interpretation of all Bible references to future punishment. If the soul cannot die, then every reference to its death or destruction must of necessity be understood to mean an intolerable existence. And, as the words used do undoubtedly admit of being so understood, the whole mass of teaching which we are to consider, the teaching of Paul and all the teaching of the Lord Jesus, on this subject, is naturally regarded as so much evidence for everlasting torment. God is "able to destroy a soul and body in hell". But according to this doctrine the soul cannot be destroyed in the literal sense, and on the same theory the resurrection body also cannot die again, therefore this text can only mean that God is able to condemn soul and body to an everlasting living death in hell.

But where is the evidence for this supposed cardinal doctrine of the faith? It is significant that the words "immortal soul" are never found in the Bible. Jesus declared that "Whosoever would save his life shall lose it, and whosoever shall lose his life for my sake and the gospel's shall save it. For what doth it profit a man, to gain the whole world, and forfeit his life? For what should a man give in exchange for his life? For whosoever shall be ashamed of me and of my words in this adulterous and sinful generation, the Son of man also shall be ashamed of him, when He cometh in the glory of His Father with the holy angels" (Mark 8:35-39). The Greek word rendered "life" by the Revisers throughout this passage is *"psuche"*; it is evidently used in a double sense. He who loses the earthly life for Christ's sake shall gain his life (or soul) in the world beyond, but he who tries to save his earthly life and the cost of unfaithfulness to Christ will lose his life in that deeper sense hereafter. What should a man give in exchange for his life, that life which will survive earthly death? But the word "immortal" is conspicuous by its absence here, and it is far from being implied by the sense. A "life" or "soul" which can be forfeited or lost does not at all naturally suggest an immortal soul, but rather the opposite. It is the non-Scriptural doctrine of the immortality of the soul which has attached the implication of endless torment to the phrase to lose one's soul. The Bible rather suggests that the man is deprived of life; or, if you will, deprived of his soul. But "soul" is to be understood in the sense of the life which is beyond the grave, as the passage in Mark plainly shows.

Paul says of God that He only has immortality (1 Timothy 6:16). But may it be (as the present writer used to think) that God, Who alone is absolutely immortal, has bestowed immortality on every human soul, so that for good or evil its existence can never end? The answer is that we must see whether His Word tells us that He has in fact done this. And there is not a single statement anywhere in the Bible to this effect!

Genesis 2:7 is sometimes quoted as though it supplied the lack. "And Jehovah God formed man of the dust of the ground, and breathed into his nostrils the breath of life; and man became a living soul". But first, there is no word of immortality here. "A living soul" is not an immortal soul". Secondly, the man who "became a living soul" was told that if he disobeyed God he should surely die, and Paul's comments on the story of the Fall (Romans 5) show that he understood that the "death" introduced by the Fall affected not the body only but the soul in the life beyond. Thirdly, the words "a living soul" almost certainly have no reference even to the truth that man survives death. The identical Hebrew words rendered "living soul" in Genesis 2:7 are rendered "living creature" in Genesis 2:19; 9:12 and elsewhere, referring to the brute creation "A living creature" would really be the most accurate rendering in Genesis 2:7 also. The fact that man survives death is certainly revealed in the Bible, but not in Genesis 2:7.

Neither in this verse nor anywhere else is there any evidence for the notion that God has given immortality to the human race. What is said is that He gives eternal life to those who believe on the Lord Jesus Christ, but this is a gift from Him to them as believers (see e.g., Romans 6:23), not something which He has ordered to be a natural possession of humanity. As regards "them that are perishing", it is said that they will have a "resurrection of judgment" ((John 5:29), but it is nowhere expressly said that they are given endless life.

One attempt to find the immortality of the soul in the Bible has already been mentioned, two more, of a different kind, may be discussed here. It is said that God made man in His own image (Genesis 1:27), which of course was a moral not a physical image. Is not immortality an essential quality of God, and must it not therefore be a part of His image? This argument fails on two grounds. First, immortality is no more an essential quality of God than omnipotence, omniscience and omnipresence, which He certainly never imparted to man. Therefore Genesis 1:27 is no ground for the idea that Adam was created immortal. We do not suggest that he was created mortal in the same sense as he was mortal after his fall. The very fact that the penalty of his sin was death shows that before he fell he was not subject to death in the sense that he could not escape it. Most probably he was so constituted that he might either become truly immortal by obedience, or become mortal by disobedience, as actually happened. In any case, his creation in the image of God tells us nothing by itself as to his immortality.

Secondly, even if the image of God did originally include immortality, man fell, and defaced the image, and it is written that Adam "begat a son in his own likeness, after his image" (Genesis 5:3). And the penalty of Adam's sin was death.

Then there is another attempt to find universal immortality in Scripture, this time in the words of our Lord. In answering the Sadducees, when they tried so confidently to perplex Him with their conundrum, our Lord said "That the dead are raised, even Moses shewed, in the place concerning the Bush, when he calleth the Lord the God of Abraham, and the God of Jacob. Now He is not the God of the dead, but of the living: for all live unto Him"

(Luke 20:37, 38). "All live unto Him" is taken by some as an assertion of universal immortality. But this is a quite impossible interpretation of our Lord's meaning. In the first place, God was indeed the God of the patriarchs, but He is not the God of those who reject Him (Hosea 1:9): and the latter cannot be said to "live unto Him". The word "all" means all whose God He truly is, the argument has no application to any others. Secondly, the whole context shows that the resurrection of which our Lord was speaking was only the "resurrection of the just". "They that are accounted worthy to attain to that world, and the resurrection from the dead, neither marry, nor are given in marriage; for neither can they die any more: for they are equal unto the angels; and are sons of God, being sons of the resurrection" (verses 35, 36). These words could not possibly apply to any but the saved. In the whole passage the unsaved are not in our Lord's mind at all, except for the implication that there are some who will not be accounted worthy to attain to that world, and to whom therefore the words "neither can they die any more" do not apply. So far from proving universal immortality, these words of our Lord suggest, though they do not conclusively prove, the contrary.

But, it may be asked, if the soul survives death, is not that in itself evidence that it is immortal? We are asked what could destroy the soul which has survived the first death. We reply that the power of Almighty God is cause enough! "Be not afraid of them which kill the body, but are not able to kill the soul: but rather fear Him which is able to destroy both soul and body in hell". These words seem to us to teach plainly that the soul, which does not perish in the first death, does perish under God's judgment, in the second death. The objection is not founded on Scripture evidence, whereas the reply to it is.

There is only one kind of Scripture evidence which can plausibly be alleged in support of universal immortality: namely those texts which are supposed to teach that the doom of the unsaved will be everlasting torment. It is agreed by all that the saved have endless life: if there were cogent evidence that the unsaved will suffer endless torment, it would obviously follow that they too have an endless existence. But the value of this evidence depends on whether those texts are rightly interpreted, and we propose to show that they do not prove everlasting torment at all. So then, the doctrine of the immortality of every soul can only be proven from Scripture, if at all, by first proving the doctrine of endless torment. Clearly then the former theory cannot be used as an argument for the latter.

Chapter 2: Will Evil Exist for Ever?

A very great difficulty (the present writer feels it to be the greatest of all) in the way of everlasting torment can be expressed in the form of a question. We do not believe that evil has existed from all eternity in the past, but can we believe that it will exist for all future eternity in hell? Will there always be an "outer darkness" outside the kingdom of God, a prison of evil co-eternal with God Himself and His redeemed?

Paul has something to say on this subject in two passages in his Epistles. In 1 Corinthians 15:24-28 he is writing of the final consummation of all things. He says that when the Lord Jesus Christ has abolished every power other than His own, and God has put all enemies under Christ's feet, then the Son will give up the kingdom to the Father, and Himself to be subjected to Him, "That God may be all in all". For our present purpose the important words are those of the concluding clause "that God may be all in all": we cannot enter here into a discussion of the difficulties raised by the preceding words, but must merely indicate our own view of their meaning. The general sense of the passage seems to be that our Lord will ultimately give up His mediatorial office, when every hostile power has been "put under His feet", and redeemed man will be in fellowship with God alone (though of course still God Triune), that God may be all in all. These words "all in all" are literally "everything in everything". There will then be no other power than that of God in the universe, and He will fill everything, and everything will be in perfect harmony with Him.

In Ephesians 1:9, 10, Paul writes of the good pleasure which God purposed in Christ "unto a dispensation of the fulness of the times, to sum up all things in Christ, the things in the heavens, and the things upon the earth". By comparing this passage with that in 1 Corinthians, we see that first all things will be summed up in Christ, then He Himself will deliver up His kingdom, and resign His office of Mediator, that God may be all in all.

But there is another passage with which these words in Ephesians should be compared, Philippians 2:9, 10. Paul says that God gave to Jesus the Name which is above every name, "that in the Name of Jesus every knee should bow, of things in heaven and things on earth and things under the earth, and that every tongue should confess that Jesus Christ is Lord, to the glory of God the Father". The "things in heaven and things on earth" are mentioned in both passages, but the "things under the earth" of Philippians are significantly absent in Ephesians. The powers of evil will be forced to own Christ's lordship, when they are put under His feet, but they cannot be "summed up" in Him. Are they then eternally to remain, still existing, but not part of the all things summed up in Christ, and exceptions to the statement that God will be "all in all"?

It must indeed be noticed that in 1 Corinthians 15 Paul speaks of putting Christ's enemies under His feet rather than of destroying them, and the Greek word for "abolish" is an ambiguous word, which may mean either "destroy" or "deprive of all power". But of course, putting His enemies under His feet does not by any means exclude their subsequent destruction. With "the last enemy that shall be abolished is "death" we may compare Revelation 20:14 "And death and Hades were cast into the lake of fire". It is clear that in Revelation the Seer is expressing symbolically the utter end of death: abstractions like death and Hades could poetically be spoken of as destroyed, but hardly as tormented, and the Seer does not in fact use this word about them.

But the question which we have to face is how God could be all in all, and how all things could be summed up in Christ, if evil were to exist eternally in hell? Would not His victory be imperfect, and above all would not His kingdom be incomplete? The demons and men in hell would be His conquered enemies, it is true, but His enemies still, with wills and desires in opposition to Him, however unable to make that opposition effective. How then could His kingdom be truly universal, and He Himself "all in all"?

There is nothing in these considerations which conflicts with the teaching of the Bible about penal suffering in the process of destruction, for in 1 Corinthians 15:28 Paul is writing of the final consummation of all things, the last event of which the Word of God has anything to say, the ultimate completion of the victory of God: "Then cometh the end". Nothing is said as to how long that end may be delayed. But it will surely come, and it seems unthinkable that after it, and to all eternity, there will still be beings hostile to God existing in His universe, still a corner of it subdued by force, and not one with Him in love.

When the present writer still believed in everlasting torment, the only answer that he could give to this difficulty was to suppose that the "outer darkness" was where to all eternity God had willed not to be, an exception by His own decree from His omnipresence, excluded from His universal kingdom. When the impossibility of this conception gradually dawned upon him, it did more than anything else to prepare his mind for the change of view to which he was brought by a re-examination of the whole subject in the Bible. In the next chapters the Biblical evidence is considered.

Chapter 3: The Meaning of the Word "Eternal"

"Depart from me, ye cursed, into the eternal fire which is prepared for the devil and his angels . . . And these shall go away into eternal punishment: but the righteous into eternal life" (Matthew 25:41, 46). The word here translated "eternal" is in Greek "*aionios*" and is uniformly rendered "eternal" in the Revised Version, but in the Authorized Version sometimes "eternal" and sometimes "everlasting". In particular, the Authorized Version has "everlasting punishment" in Matthew 25:46. But the question we have now to consider is whether "aionios" or "eternal" is really the same in meaning as "everlasting", as the Authorized Version translators evidently supposed; and especially whether "eternal punishment" really means endless conscious suffering, which the translation "everlasting punishment" certainly suggests.

It is easy to show from the phrase "eternal life", which is found 43 times out of the 70 occurrences of "eternal" in the New Testament, that "eternal" is more than merely endless or everlasting. There is a difference in kind as well as in duration between the eternal and the earthly. The believer has eternal life at the same time as the earthly life which must end in death (John 5:24), and in 1 Timothy 6 that which is called "eternal life" in verse 12 is called "life that is life indeed" in verse 19 (R.V.).

But though "eternal" is more than endless, the idea of permanence is an essential part of it. Eternal life is certainly endless: see e.g., John 3:16; 11:26. But perhaps the clearest evidence that the idea of permanence is inherent in the word is to be found in 2 Corinthians 4:17-5:1. "For our light affliction, which is for the moment, worketh for us more and more exceedingly an eternal weight of glory; while we look not at the things which are seen, but at the things which are not seen: for the things which are seen are temporal; but the things which are not seen are eternal. For we know that if the earthly house of our tabernacle be dissolved, we have a building from God, a house not made with hands, eternal, in the heavens." It is clear that the word "eternal" is used here as the opposite of "temporal", "for the moment", "earthly". The permanence of eternity is contrasted with the transience of earthly things. So also the "eternal tabernacles" of Luke 16:9 are contrasted with the uncertain duration of earthly riches. Let it be granted that "eternal" is a word of quality rather than of mere duration, yet permanence is an essential part of that quality.

Leaving aside for the present the 7 instances where the word is used with words of judgment and punishment, in 58 out of the remaining 63 places (including the 43 of "eternal life") it is associated with beings or things which we all know to be endless, such as God Himself, Christ's kingdom, our salvation and the like (see Luke 16:9; Romans 16:26; 2 Corinthians 4:17-5:1; 1 Timothy 6:16; 2 Timothy 2:10; Hebrews 5:9; Hebrews 9:12, 14, 15, 13:20; 1 Peter 5:10; 2 Peter 1:11; Revelation 14:6). The 5 remaining instances include three examples of the phrase "before times eternal", in reference to the ages of past eternity. God "called us with a holy calling . . . according to His own purpose and grace, which was given us in Christ Jesus before times eternal" (2 Timothy 1:9). God's purposes are as eternal as He is Himself, and no limitation of time can be intended here. "Eternal life, which God, Who cannot lie, promised before times eternal" (Titus 1:2). These words could be understood of the Old Testament prophecies, in which case of course "eternal" must have a relative and limited meaning, like "in past ages". But the use of the phrase "before times eternal" in 2 Timothy 1:9 most probably determines its meaning here. Eternal life was promised in the counsels of God from all eternity. For, God's plan of salvation had been in His mind from eternity, but as we are told in Romans 16:25, 26, had been "kept in silence through times eternal" (i.e., through the ages of eternity), till it was made known through the Old Testament prophets and later through the preaching of Jesus Christ. No limitation of time can be intended here. Then there is the phrase "eternal comfort" (2 Thessalonians 2:16), where the meaning seems to be a comfort which survives death and goes on through the ages of eternity. Lastly there is a remarkable use of the word in the Epistle to Philemon. "For perhaps he (*Onesimus*) was therefore parted from thee for a season, that thou shouldest have him for ever (*aionion*); no longer as a servant, but . . . a brother beloved . . . both in the flesh and in the Lord" (Philemon 15, 16). Some have taken "for ever" or "eternally" here to mean no more than "for the rest of thy life", which indeed is not impossible in the familiar language of a personal note, just as we might in like case write "for always". But it is at least equally possible, and more in keeping with the general usage of the word in Scripture, that Paul meant quite literally "for ever". Philemon's fellowship with Onesimus "in the flesh" would end at death, but "in the Lord" would continue through all eternity. Of all the instances where "eternal" is used with a word not implying judgment or punishment, this example in a private letter is the only case in the New Testament where a limited sense of the word has any considerable probability: and even here the unlimited sense is possible, and in our view the more likely to have been Paul's meaning.

The seven examples of "eternal" with words of judgment and punishment must now be considered.

1. "It is good for thee to enter into life maimed or halt, rather than having two hands or two feet to be cast into eternal fire" (Matthew 18:8).

2. This verse belongs to a passage which is parallel to Mark 9:43-48, where the phrase is "unquenchable fire".

3. "Depart from me, ye cursed, into the eternal fire which is prepared for the devil and his angels . . . And these shall go away into eternal punishment, but the righteous into eternal life" (Matthew 25:41, 46).

4. "Sodom and Gomorrah and the cities about them . . . are set forth as an example, suffering the punishment of eternal fire" (Jude 7).

5. "Whosoever shall blaspheme against the Holy Spirit hath never forgiveness, but is guilty of an eternal sin" (Mark 3:29 R.V.).

6. In Hebrews 6:2 "eternal judgment" is mentioned as one of the "first principles of Christ".

7. In 2 Thessalonians 1:9 Paul says that they who know not God and obey not the gospel of the Lord Jesus "shall suffer punishment, even eternal destruction from the face of the Lord and from the glory of His might".

There are then three instances of "eternal fire", and one each of "an eternal sin", "eternal punishment", "eternal judgment", "eternal destruction". It might seem at first as though the results of our previous study of the word "eternal" point straight to the doctrine of everlasting torment, for we have seen that whatever else "eternal" may mean, the idea of permanence is an essential part of its meaning. But here there is an important point to be noticed. In six of its seventy uses in the New Testament, the word "eternal" is used with words meaning acts of processes, as distinct from persons or things, and of these four are included in the seven which we are now studying. The six acts or processes are:

- salvation (Hebrews 5:9)
- redemption (Hebrews 9:12)
- judgment (Hebrews 6:2)
- sin (Mark 3:29)
- punishment (Matthew 25:46)
- destruction (2 Thessalonians 1:9)

Now it is clear that the first four of these words can only be eternal in the sense that their results are so. Eternal salvation or redemption is not completed in this life, the process is to be completed definitely and finally in "the day of redemption" (Ephesians 4:30), the salvation is "ready to be revealed in the last time" (1 Peter 1:5). Nor would anyone suppose that eternal judgment means a judgment eternally being pronounced, or that when our Lord called the blasphemy against the Holy Spirit an eternal sin He meant that it was a sin eternally repeated. It is the effects of the salvation, the judgment and the sin which are eternal.

Therefore it is at least possible – may we not say, probable? – that eternal punishment and eternal destruction should be interpreted in the same way, i.e., not as an eternally continued punishment or destruction, but rather as a punishment or destruction eternal in its effects. Compare Psalm 92:7: "When all the workers of iniquity do flourish, it is that they shall be destroyed for ever". Earthly punishment can at most destroy the body, and is not eternal, for there will be a resurrection: But He who destroys soul and body in hell destroys with an eternal destruction from which there is no resurrection. In 2 Thessalonians 1:9 "punishment" and "destruction" are combined, though the word for "punishment" is not the same as that used in Matthew 25:46. The persecutors of God's people "shall suffer punishment, even eternal destruction (proceeding) from the face of the Lord and from the glory of His might".

It is often argued that since "eternal punishment" and "eternal life" are found in the same verse (Matthew 25:46), the word "eternal must mean the same in both. That argument has force against any theory of ultimate restoration. The results of the punishment must be as eternal, which includes the idea of permanence, as eternal life itself. An eternal punishment which could end in restoration would be as much a contradiction in terms as an eternal life which could end in death. But eternal life is an eternal state, and an eternal state must be a permanent one: but punishment is an act or process, and therefore the analogy of the usage elsewhere suggests a punishment with eternal results, which would be the case if the punishment consisted in ending the person's existence to all eternity.

There remains, however, the phrase "eternal fire", elsewhere described as "unquenchable fire". Fire is a thing, and not an act, therefore we should certainly expect that "eternal fire" should mean "fire which burns for ever", the more so as it is also called "unquenchable" fire. But Jude 7 throws doubt on this interpretation: "Sodom and Gomorrah, and the cities about them . . . are set forth as an example, suffering the punishment of eternal fire". This cannot mean that the fire which destroyed the cities is eternally burning, for such is not the case, nor was it in Jude's day. Are we then to understand that it is the inhabitants of the cities who are suffering the punishment of eternal fire in hell? But the punishment of those people in hell could not be described as an example, for living people, who alone could profit by the example, could not know of it. Moreover, our Lord said that it would be more tolerable for Sodom and Gomorrah in the day of judgment, than for those cities which had heard and seen Him, and yet had not accepted Him. This hardly seems compatible with the idea that their punishment in the next life is of exemplary severity. But what actually happened to Sodom and Gomorrah was that they were destroyed by fire and brimstone from Jehovah out of heaven, never to all eternity to be inhabited again. Thus in Jude 7 the interpretation "fire which destroys for ever" or "fire with eternal results" gives a sense which corresponds accurately with the facts, and seems to be the only possible meaning.[1] This may not be the true interpretation of "eternal fire" in Matthew 18:8 and 25:41. There the meaning is probably governed by that of Mark 9:43-48, which will be examined later (see Chapter 5). The conclusion of the discussion there is that the "unquenchable fire" represents a perpetual memorial of God's righteous judgment, which continues for ever after the existence of the condemned has ended. But a meaning clearly appropriate in Jude 7 cannot be altogether ruled out as impossible in Matthew.

The results of our enquiry may be summed up as follows. The sense of permanence is an essential part of the meaning of "eternal", as much in its application to judgment and punishment as in its other uses. But the permanence seems to be attached to the results of the acts or processes themselves. If so, the way is left open to the view that eternal punishment may mean a punishment which ends for ever the existence of the persons punished. We do not claim to have proved that this interpretation is certainly right, but to have shown that it is legitimate and possible, and cannot (so far as the texts

---

[1] The alternative translation in the R.V. margin is "are set forth as an example of eternal fire, suffering punishment". This is grammatically possible, though it makes the words "suffering punishment" somewhat pointless. But it would agree well with the interpretation suggested above. The total and final destruction of the cities would then be set forth as an example of what eternal fire in hell does.

containing the word "eternal" are concerned) be called a forcing of Scripture to suit a theory.

Chapter 4: The General Trend of Bible Teaching

The foregoing study of the word "eternal" has given results which are decidedly against theories of the Ultimate Restoration of the lost. But neither Matthew 25:46 nor any other text containing the word "eternal" can be used either as proof of the doctrine of everlasting torment, or as decisive evidence against it. On the other hand, there are certain passages, not more than four in all (Matthew 18:34, 35; Mark 9:43-38; Revelation 14:10, 11; 20:10), the first obvious meaning of which does seem to point to an everlasting continuance of conscious suffering in hell for those who are sent there. But before considering whether this first obvious meaning of these passages is necessarily the true meaning, it is well to see what the general teaching of the New Testament on this subject apart from them. We propose, therefore, to reserve the consideration of these four passages to the next chapter. In order to avoid undue repetition, the reader is asked to note that in the present chapter all general statements about New Testament teaching are to be understood as excepting those four passages.

Separation From God: Penal Suffering

Some texts emphasize the separation from God of those who are condemned at the Judgment. "Depart from me, ye that work iniquity" (Matthew 7:23; cp. Luke 13:27). The same thought is expressed by "the outer darkness" (Matthew 8:12; 22:13; 25:30). Compare also Jude 13 "wandering stars, for whom the blackness of darkness has been reserved for ever". Here, however, the thought may not be exclusion from God only, but also the end of existence: the wandering stars are extinguished in eternal night. 2 Peter 2:17, which omits the figure "wandering stars" also omits "for ever".

Other texts speak of suffering, but without any indication of duration. The "outer darkness" texts quoted above contain the terrible phrase "there shall be the weeping and gnashing of teeth".

The same phrase occurs also in Matthew 13:42, 50; 24:51; Luke 13:28. In none of these texts is there any statement that the suffering will continue for ever, and indeed, as we shall see presently, the first two rather suggest the contrary. The parable of the Rich Man and Lazarus seems to refer to the time between death and the judgment. It is, therefore, outside the scope of this book, and we shall not discuss it.

Paul, who generally speaks only of "destruction" or "perdition" as the fate of the wicked, in one place uses the words "tribulation and anguish" (Romans 2:9).

Penal suffering, therefore, certainly forms a part of Bible teaching about the doom of the lost, but there is no statement that this suffering will continue for ever.

Fire

Then there are those passages which speak of fire. Again it is to be noticed that none of the texts that speak of fire say that the lost will suffer eternally in it. The nearest approach to such a statement is the mention of the "eternal fire" (Matthew 18:8; 25:41), the meaning of which, from the analogy of Jude 7, may be "the fire which destroys for ever", even as the fire from heaven destroyed Sodom and Gomorrah for ever. But see the discussion of this phrase in the previous chapter.

But we can go further than this. The main emphasis in the texts that speak of fire is on the destructive rather than the tormenting effects of the fire, John the Baptist says of the Lord Jesus that "He will gather His wheat into the garner, but the chaff He will burn up, with unquenchable fire" (Matthew 3:12, Luke 3:17). The Greek word rendered "burn up", like its English equivalent, is a strong word implying total destruction, and chaff is utterly destroyed by fire. The word "unquenchable" means simply "that which nothing and no one can quench", which cannot be prevented from accomplishing its destructive purpose. But there may be the further thought that, after it has completed the destruction, it continues for ever as a memorial of the wrath of God (see additional note on

Chapter 5). In any case it can hardly be intended to reverse the meaning of "burn up" by suggesting an eternally *uncompleted* process of burning.

The wicked are compared by John the Baptist and our Lord to a tree which is hewn down and cast into the fire (Matthew 3:10; 7:19). So also John 15:6: "If a man abide not in me, he is cast forth as a branch, and is withered; and they gather them, and cast them into the fire, and they are burned". It is the destruction of what is worthless that the imagery suggests, not endless torment of living beings. Twice in the Epistles the destruction of the wicked by fire is spoken of: "A fierceness of fire which shall devour the adversaries" (Hebrews 10:27); "the revelation of the Lord Jesus from heaven with the angels of His power in flaming fire, rendering vengeance to them that know not God, and to them that obey not the gospel of our Lord Jesus: who shall suffer punishment, even eternal destruction from the face of the Lord and from the glory of His might" (2 Thessalonians 1:7-9).

In fact there are only three places in the New Testament where the fire of hell is clearly and unmistakably associated with penal suffering. In Matthew 25:41 the condemned are told to "depart . . . into the eternal fire which is prepared for the devil and his angels", and it is said later, "And these shall go away into eternal punishment". We have seen that the usage of the word "eternal" at least permits, and we would say supports, the view that the "eternal fire"[2] inflicts a punishment which is eternal because it finally destroys. In the other two places, though penal suffering is indicated, the destruction of what is worthless is the more prominent idea. In the Parable of the Tares we read, "As, therefore, the tares are gathered up and burned with fire; so shall it be in the end of the world" (Matthew 13:40). Our Lord adds that the Son of Man will send forth His angels, and they shall cast the wicked into the furnace of fire, "there shall be the weeping and gnashing of teeth". And in verses 47-50 of the same chapter, the Parable of the Drag Net tells how the fishermen gather the good fish into vessels, and cast away the bad. "So shall it be in the end of the world: the

---

[2] See Chapter 3.

angels shall come forth, and sever the wicked from among the righteous, and shall cast them into the furnace of fire: there shall be weeping and gnashing of teeth". These terrible words do make quite clear that the destruction is not immediate, and that the purpose of the fire is not to consume only. But they do not remove the impression of the imagery that the wicked are compared to the worthless weeds which are thrown into the fire to be burned up, and to the worthless fish which are thrown away to be got rid of. Penal suffering comes into the application of the parables, for a death by fire is necessarily a very awful death, but it surely is not the main point, or it could not be so entirely lacking in the imagery of the parables themselves.

But what of the lake of fire in the Book of Revelation? It is mentioned four times (19:20; 20:10, 14; 21:8). The second of these is among the four passages which we are reserving for later consideration. Revelation 21:8 ends with these words, "Their part shall be in the lake that burneth[3] with fire and brimstone, which is the second death". The term which the Seer is explaining here is not the second death, but the lake of fire. Compare "seven horns and seven eyes, which are the seven Spirits of God" (v. 6), and "bowls full of incense, which are the prayers of the saints" (5:8), and "for the fine linen is the righteous acts of the saints" (19:8). It is clear that the horns and eyes, the bowls of incense and the fine linen are symbols which are explained in the second half of each clause. So here the lake of fire is the symbol, and the second death that which explains it. Revelation 20:14 is more ambiguously expressed, "Death and Hades were cast into the lake of fire. This is the second death, even the lake of fire". But comparison with 21:8 shows that the meaning is, "This symbol, the lake of fire, is the second death". But if the "second death" is the explanation of the symbol "the lake of fire", this explanation should surely have its natural meaning, and so the suggestion of these phrases is that the second death is indeed a very awful death, a fiery death, but, nevertheless, ultimately *death*, death of the soul as well as the body (Matthew 10:28).

---

[3] The same strong word is used in the Greek, as that which is translated "burn up" in Matthew 3:12.

Death, Destruction, Perish

We have seen that the majority of those texts which speak of the fire of hell seem to lay the main emphasis on the destroying and consuming function of fire, even where the thought of suffering is not absent. Now we must consider those texts which use such words as "destruction", "perdition", "consume", "perish", for the doom of the lost. In our Lord's own teaching these are Matthew 10:28, "Fear Him which is able to destroy both soul and body in hell; Matthew 21:44, "He that falleth on this stone shall be broken to pieces, but on whomsoever it shall fall, it will scatter him as dust"; Luke 13:3, "Except ye repent, ye shall all in like manner perish" (it is possible, but not at all likely, that our Lord means bodily death here); Luke 19:27, "These mine enemies, which would not that I should reign over them, bring hither and slay them before me"; and John 3:16 (which *may* be the inspired comment of the Evangelist rather than the direct words of the Lord), "God so loved the world that He gave His only begotten Son, that whosoever believeth in Him should not perish, but have eternal life".

In the *Acts* not much is said which bears on future punishment. Peter says to Simon Magnus, "Thy money perish (lit. be for perdition) with thee" (8:20): the rejecters of the Gospel "perish" (13:41); they "judge themselves unworthy of eternal life" (13:46); their blood will be on their own heads (18:6). Compare Paul's words to the elders of Ephesus, "I am pure from the blood of all men" (20:26), meaning that he had given his witness faithfully, so that none would perish through his default.

In the Epistles, future punishment is almost invariably referred to in terms of death and destruction. Penal suffering is mentioned twice only: "tribulation and anguish" (Romans 2:9), and "affliction" (2 Thessalonians 1:6). There is no suggestion in these passages that the suffering will be everlasting, but in 2 Thessalonians 1:9, Paul speaks of eternal destruction, the meaning of which we have considered above. Those who are without Christ in this life are four times spoken of as "they that are perishing" (1 Corinthians 1:18; 2 Corinthians 2:15; 4:3; 2 Thessalonians 2:10).

Other striking expressions are, "the wages of sin is death" (Romans 6:23); "if ye live after the flesh, ye must die" (Romans 8:13); "whose end is perdition" (Philippians 3:19); "hurtful lusts, such as drown men in destruction and perdition" (1 Timothy 6:9); "sin, when it is full grown, bringeth forth death" (James 1:15); "the day of judgment and destruction of ungodly men" (2 Peter 3:7).

Summary of Teaching So Far Considered

The general trend of the Bible teaching so far considered, is that those whom God condemns at the final judgment will be separated for ever from Him, and sentenced to a very awful "second death". But just as in the language of this world a "terrible death" means a death accompanied by suffering and horror, but yet is quite definitely the end of life, so the texts so far considered supply no reason why the second death should not be the end of existence, although it will be a terrible death, a death by fire, whatever the "fire" may mean.

The fire is spoken of chiefly as that which burns up or devours those whom God has rejected as unfit for the gift of eternal life. The fact that they must suffer in the process of destruction is undoubtedly a part of the Bible teaching, but it is less prominently or frequently stated than the fact that their doom is destruction. Throughout the Epistles, from Romans to Jude, there is only one passage which refers to future punishment without using some word meaning "die" or "destroy" or "perish", and that one (Romans 2:9) speaks of "tribulation and anguish", but without any suggestion that it is eternally continued.

The Meaning of "Death" and Destruction

We are well aware of the reasons which have been put forward to show that such words as "death", "destruction", and the like are capable of a meaning other than the end of existence. They are and we have no thought of disputing it. For example, those who reject Christ are said to be "dead in trespasses and sins" even in this life (Ephesians 2:1, and see Luke 9:60): they have life, but not true life. So also the Greek words rendered in the active "destroy" and in the passive "perish" or "be lost", and this verb and the derived nouns are quite often used with reference to a ruined and useless condition of a person or thing.

But it is possible to press this fact too far, true as it is. It is not denied that, *if* it were clear beyond question from Bible teaching elsewhere that the doom of the lost will be everlasting torment, it would be quite possible to understand "death", "destruction" and the like, as meaning a wretched and ruined existence. But we have now considered the whole body of Bible teaching on this subject, except four passages, and the weight of the evidence has been against everlasting torment rather than for it. Moreover the context generally indicates clearly enough when those words are to be understood in this secondary sense. The disciples say, "to what purpose hath this waste of the ointment been made?" (Mark 14:4), where "waste" represents the word elsewhere rendered "perdition". But the context indicates plainly the sense in which the word is used. The same is true of "Leave the dead to bury their own dead" or "dead in trespasses and sins". But there is no context to suggest that "whose end is perdition" (Philippians 3:19), or "a fierceness of fire which shall destroy the adversaries" (Hebrews 10:27) are intended to mean an eternity of conscious torment, rather than the destruction of which they appear to speak. And this is true not only of the context of the texts themselves, but also there is no positive evidence for everlasting torment in the whole of the Epistles from Romans to Jude. The nearest approach to an exception is the phrase "eternal destruction" in 2 Thessalonians 1:9; but, as we have seen, the meaning of other similar phrases, such as "eternal judgment", "eternal salvation", "an eternal sin", does not at all support the view that "eternal destruction" means an eternally continued process of destruction.

Seeing then that the Epistles are the chief source from which all, or nearly all, Christian doctrines are derived, it is very strange that, if the true doctrine which the Word of God intends us to receive is that of everlasting torment, there should be no clear statement of it anywhere in the Epistles, but that they should always use terms which seem on the face of them to point to the end of existence. We have seen that our Lord's teaching the greater number of His sayings point in the same direction, and only in two of His sayings (or three, if Matthew 25:41, 46 be counted) is there even any appearance of teaching everlasting torment. Is not this a strong reason for hoping the first impression given by those two sayings, which we have not yet considered, will be found not to be the true meaning; as we have seen reason for believing in the case of the verses in Matthew 25?

Additional Note to Chapter 4

Is the Scripture Ambiguous?

Dr. Agar Beet in *The Last Things* put forward with great learning and ability the view that, as between endless torment and the ultimate ending of existence, the teaching of the Bible is ambiguous. Neither view is ruled out, neither can be held to be definitely proved from the Bible. Dr. Beet builds this theory on what we regard as the secondary meaning of the words "death", "destruction", "perdition" and the like, which for him is the essential meaning. He says that these words certainly do not of themselves mean endless torment, but neither on the other hand do they mean ultimate extinction of existence. "Destruction" or "perdition", he says means utter and final ruin, but indicates nothing as to what becomes of the ruined person or object: it is compatible with either a continued miserable existence, or a cessation of existence, but it proves neither. So also, "death" in his view is the deprivation of all that makes life worth living, but not necessarily the end of existence, though it might be, if there were other conclusive evidence, which, however he says there is not. In sum, he holds that God has not seen fit to reveal to us clearly and certainly what the ultimate fate of the wicked will be, beyond the fact that it will be irretrievable and utter ruin.

On this theory the present writer has three observations to make. First, although we grant freely that words such as "destroy" or "death" quite frequently have the meaning of "ruin" or "deprivation of good life", yet we cannot admit that this is any but a secondary use, the primary sense being "deprive of existence" and "end of existence". And there are definite reasons which show that the use of these words in the New Testament, as applied to future punishment, is not so vague and indeterminate as Dr. Beet supposes. Here are two of these reasons.

1. The terms "life" and "death". Put together these three facts.
   (a) There is no statement in the Bible that all men are immortal, but on the contrary a definite statement that only God has immortality:
   (b) there are many express statements that eternal life is the gift of God through Jesus Christ:
   (c) Paul says that "the wages of sin is death". Surely the natural suggestion of these three facts taken together is that death means not only the deprivation of a happy existence, but what it naturally should mean in human language, the end of existence. This natural suggestion is not in itself final proof, but we submit that it is *prima facie* evident, which requires something definite on the other side to overthrow it. In other words "death" is not merely neutral, it has a strong bias in the direction of the end of existence.

2. The term "destroy". The Greek word is very often used in the sense of "ruin", and we do not deny that it can be ambiguous. But we deny that this word is always or generally ambiguous, as applied to future punishment in the New Testament.

Dr. Beet says that we must not put too much weight on the one metaphor of the destruction of vegetable matter (i.e., chaff, weeds, branches) by fire. But we submit that the life of *any* living thing is necessarily ended by fire, unless God supernaturally provides otherwise: therefore, where fire is in question, the verb "destroy" is not ambiguous at all, but definitely implies the ending of life. It would be ridiculous to say that any living thing was thrown into the fire to be "ruined". God is able to destroy soul and body in hell (Matthew 10:28). Now hell is a place of fire: the word Gehenna is rarely used without some mention of fire in the context. To destroy in hell means to destroy by fire. So also again, when the writer to the Hebrews says that fire shall devour the adversaries (10:27), the natural meaning of the words is certainly that their life will be ended, and of course not their bodily life alone, but body and soul, as our Lord said. Only one thing would upset this conclusion, and that is definite evidence that all souls are immortal, and therefore cannot be destroyed (in the full sense of the word) even by fire. But there is no such evidence, as Dr. Beet acknowledges.

Our second observation is that if the words "death" and "destroy" are used in a neutral sense of "ruin", and prove nothing either way as between endless torment and ultimate extinction, this ambiguity must have been deliberately intended by God. We should have to suppose that the inspiring Spirit did not reveal to the Apostles any more exact information about the fate of the condemned than that it would be a final ruin. If Paul, for instance, had known that they would suffer in torment for all eternity, it is incredible that he should have been content to use terms by which he meant nothing more definite than "ruin", or an ambiguous "death", which could be understood equally well as endless misery or the cessation of existence. But as regards the Lord Jesus, Who knew all the facts of the other world, we should be compelled to suppose that He deliberately used ambiguous language.

This takes us straight to our third observation, which is that Dr. Beet's theory must logically issue in ruling out endless torment as quite incredible. The Lord Jesus certainly knew the full truth. If that truth were that the condemned would ultimately come to the end of their existence, then His use of terms which men have misunderstood, largely through the influence of a theory of immortality of the soul, which He did *not* teach, is natural enough. But if the truth were endless torment, what then? If God is really going to punish those who reject salvation with endless torments, it is unbelievable that He should not have inspired His Apostles to tell men so in unmistakable terms, while there is still time for repentance. It is also unthinkable that His Son, foreseeing so awful a fate for the impenitent, should have contented Himself with the veiled hints which fall far short of warning them in advance. The advocate of the traditional theory is here on far stronger ground than Dr. Beet, for the former interprets our Lord's words as giving very distinct warnings of this awful fate, and he maintains that He did this in His love and pity, if so be that men might be warned in time.

Indeed this theory of Dr. Beet rules out endless torment in two ways.

> First, it enormously increases the moral difficulty of believing that God could punish his creatures with endless torment, by adding the supposition that having formed this purpose He deliberately refrained from warning men clearly what He intends to do.

> Secondly, the doctrine of endless torment is by common consent so dreadful, that only a deep conviction that the teaching of the Bible cannot honestly be explained otherwise, can make it possible to believe that God could punish so. Such a doctrine cannot be accepted at all as a mere 'perhaps". If there is doubt, the doubt must be resolved on the side of the more merciful theory.

Chapter 5: The Four Excepted Passages

We now approach the study of the four passages, which we reserved to the last on the ground that they have the appearance of being exceptions to the general trend of the Scripture teaching in that the first impression which they give is in favour of the doctrine of everlasting torment. Two of the four sayings of our Lord (Matthew 18:34, 35; Mark 9:43-48), and two are found in the Book of Revelation (Revelation 14:10, 11; 20:10). In the consideration of these passages there are two things to be borne in mind.

> First, they are as much the Word of God as any other Scripture, and nothing whatever can justify a dishonest wresting of their meaning. But,

> Secondly, we are entitled to take into account the general sense of the teaching of the Bible itself on this subject, and to study them with this in mind.

The second of these considerations does not by any means nullify the first. Perhaps the best way of making clear what we mean by taking into account the general sense of Scripture is to illustrate from another case where this has to be done.

The first impression which the Parable of the Unjust Steward makes on many people is that our Lord is represented as commending a dishonest action. It is of course incredible that He can really have done so, but the question might arise whether the report of His words had that meaning, in which case it could not be a true report. But in all our Lord's recorded teaching elsewhere there is nothing whatever to give any ground for supposing that those who reported His words and acts would imagine Him capable of commending dishonesty. Indeed in the words that immediately follow the parable itself, He is represented as inculcating the necessity of a faithful use of money entrusted to us. This fact legitimately supplies a very strong presumption against the truth of that first impression of His words in the Parable of the Unjust Steward. This presumption would not justify any twisting of words into a forced meaning, but it does suggest a close examination of the words used and their connection with their context. When this is done, it is seen that so far from being a commendation of dishonesty, the parable is a lesson on the wise and faithful use of money by the Christian.

In the same way, the seeming discord between the four passages which we are now about to study and the general sense of Scripture teaching on the subject elsewhere creates a strong presumption that the first impression which these passages give is not their true meaning, and suggests the need of a very careful study of them in order to get below the surface, and make sure, as far as we can, that we understand the real intention of the words.

Matthew 18:34, 35

The Parable of the Unmerciful Servant ends with the words, "And his lord was wroth, and delivered him to the tormentors, till he should pay all that was due. So shall also my heavenly Father do unto you, if ye forgive not every one his brother from your hearts". We may take together with these words another saying in Matthew 5:26: "Thou shalt by no means come out from thence (from prison) till thou have paid the last farthing". This saying indeed states nothing about torment, and, taken by itself, could not fairly be considered to suggest it: but those who believe that everlasting torment is proved by other evidence would naturally interpret this saying in conformity, for the prison is a metaphor which might cover much.

The debt owed by man to God is evidently a symbol of sin, and to pay that debt to the last farthing can mean nothing less than to suffer the full penalty that sin deserves. But when can the sinner pay in full the penalty due to his sin, represented in figures by the enormous sum of two million pounds (Matthew 18:24), *and be free*? The only possible answer is, Never. One indeed paid it for him in full, but if he rejects Him, he can certainly never pay it himself.

So far all is clear. But neither of these sayings can be made into evidence for everlasting torment without assuming something which is not said in either case, namely that the existence of the sinner must continue for ever. The illustrations used by our Lord do not suggest such a thing. A prisoner who never comes out of prison does not live there eternally. The slave who was delivered to the tormenters till he should pay two million pounds would not escape from them by payment, but he would assuredly die in the end: why should not the same result be at least a possibility in the application? The only thing which could rule out the possibility would be the definite certainty that no human soul can ever die in the full sense of the word. But it has been shown that there is no Scriptural evidence for this idea, unless it be in the doctrine of everlasting torment itself, which would then need to be proved by independent evidence, or the reasoning would be circular.

Therefore the conclusion with regard to both these parabolic statements is that their main teaching is the impossibility of the sinner ever satisfying the Divine justice and so becoming free, but that though they would agree with the doctrine of everlasting torment, if that were established elsewhere, they cannot of themselves prove it.

Mark 9:43-48

In this, the most terrible of our Lord's saying about future punishment, we are warned against clinging to anything which may cause us to stumble. Though it be as dear or seemingly necessary to us as a hand or foot or eye, it must be given up, for it is better to enter into life without it, than with it to be cast into hell, into the unquenchable fire, "where their worm dieth not, and the fire is not quenched". The first impression made by these words is that of unending torment. They suggest a process of corruption and burning, which is perpetually continuing and never completed. And as it is generally regarded as an axiom that neither the soul nor the resurrected body can ever come to an end, the assumption is made that these words are pictures of perpetual conscious suffering, whether purely spiritual, or both spiritual and physical.

But we must observe that our Lord is drawing His imagery from Isaiah 66:24. Now it would not be true to say that, when Old Testament texts are quoted in the New Testament, they are always used in exactly the sense which they have in their Old Testament setting. But there is always a presumption that a quotation has the same meaning as in its original context, and the words should not be interpreted differently in the two places without good reason.

In Isaiah 66:24 the prophet, who had been speaking of the final destruction of the enemies of Jehovah at Jerusalem says, "And they (those who come to worship) shall go forth, and look upon the carcases of the men that have transgressed against me: for their worm shall not die, neither shall their fire be quenched: and they shall be an abhorring unto all flesh". Here the picture is of a miraculously protracted destruction of *corpses*. We may say indeed that such a picture must be ideal and symbolical, and so no doubt it is; but symbolical of what? Is it a natural interpretation of symbolism to make the perpetually protracted destruction of dead bodies symbolize the perpetual torment of living souls and bodies? There seems no adequate reason for supposing that our Lord intended so to change the meaning of the prophet's words when he adopted them.

The words "they shall be an abhorring to all flesh" point to the effect of the judgment. The spectacle of corpses (which of course cannot suffer) in a perpetual process of corruption and burning would create horror and loathing in all who beheld, so in the fulfilment of the symbol we can see a perpetual memorial of the righteous wrath of God, and of His judgment against sin. May not this be the key to the meaning of our Lord's words in Mark 9?

It is clear that there will be penal suffering, for that which goes into the fire in the first instance will be alive, and therefore must suffer: "rather than having thy two hands to go into hell, into the unquenchable fire . . . rather than having two eyes to go into hell". But the question is what is meant by the added words "where their worm dieth not, and the fire is not quenched"? The comparison with the text of Isaiah seems to show that our Lord is warning those who cling to evil that their fate will be not only to perish by fire, but to become thereafter an eternal memorial of God's judgment. Like the chaff and the weeds and the dead branches, the wicked will be utterly destroyed as by fire, but the awful picture of corpses consumed by the undying worm and the unquenchable fire symbolizes that by some means there will be a perpetual memorial of that destruction which the wrath of God against sin will have achieved. Our Lord's words no more suggest the perpetual existence of human beings in conscious torment than the corpses in Isaiah's picture suggest such a thing.

It will be said that by this interpretation our Lord's warning is deprived of most of its awfulness. It is true that it is deprived of that element which has made the words so terrible a burden on the faith and conscience of those who humbly accept His authority. But to say that what remains is not so very dreadful seems to us strange blindness! Death by fire is a very terrible thing in this world, and in the timeless conditions of eternity it is only to be expected that that which corresponds to death by fire would be far more dreadful, even though death in the fullest sense were the ultimate issue. Moreover, even in this life it is a strong human instinct to desire to leave behind some honourable memorial of ourselves. We all regard the death penalty as enormously increased in horror when it is accompanied by shame and the handing down of an evil memory. Jude evidently considered that the severity of the judgment on Sodom and Gomorrah was immensely increased by the fact that they were not only destroyed, but destroyed by "eternal fire"; i.e., by fire which made them a perpetual desolation, and an eternal memorial of God's judgment on atrocious wickedness. The contrast which God puts before us in His Word is between eternal life with Him in glory, and the destruction of soul and body by fire of His wrath followed by an eternal memorial of dishonour (see Isaiah 66:24; Daniel 12:2)

If the above interpretation of Mark 9:43-48 is right, there is *no* word of the Lord Jesus Christ which teaches endless torment. There are indeed only three sayings of His which have even the appearance of teaching it; this passage in Mark, the saying at the end of the parable of the Unmerciful Servant (Matthew 18:34, 35), and the saying about eternal fire and eternal punishment (Matthew 25:41, 46). His other sayings can only be understood in that sense, if the interpretation is influence by the belief that it is impossible that any soul should really die.

Far be it from us to minimize the dreadful severity of His words. He spoke of an outer darkness, where shall be weeping and gnashing of teeth; His comparison of the condemned to weeds thrown into the furnace to be burned up indicates a final rejection and a terrible end; the imagery of the undying worm and unquenchable fire indicates that in and after their destruction the wicked will be a perpetual memorial of God's just judgment, instead of being, as they might have been, to the eternal praise of the glory of His grace (see Ephesians 1:6; 2:7). His words leave, as far as can be seen, no ray of hope that the mercy which the condemned have rejected here will ever be offered to them hereafter. But in all this there is no word to say that their suffering will be prolonged to all eternity, and even in Mark 9:43-48 the imagery is taken from the destruction of corpses which cannot feel.

Revelation 14:10, 11

"If any man worshippeth the beast and his image . . . he also shall drink of the wine of the wrath of God . . . and he shall be tormented[4] with fire and brimstone in the presence of the holy angels, and in the presence of the Lamb: and the smoke of their torment goeth up for ever and ever (Greek, unto ages of ages); and they have no rest day and night[5], they that worship the beast and his image, and whoso receiveth the mark of his name."

These words are very terrible. The Redeemer (for the title "the Lamb" refers to His redeeming death) will Himself command and approve the dreadful punishment of those who have rejected Him and His redemption, and deliberately chosen the service of His

---

[4] Matthew 5:25, 26 speaks of imprisonment, but not of torment.
[5] The phrase "day and night" is transferred from earthly to eternal conditions: it is used elsewhere of the praises of the redeemed . . . (Revelation 4:8; 7:14, 15).

enemy. The people spoken of are those who deliberately take the devil's side in the supreme contests of good and evil, when the issues are perfectly plain. But are we to understand that the torment will continue for ever and ever? This is certainly the first impression given by the words. But let us examine more closely the two clauses which give that impression. The words "they have no rest day and night" certainly say that there will be no break or intermission in the suffering of the followers of the Beast, *while it continues*: but in themselves they do not say that it will continue for ever. The words "the smoke of their torment goeth up unto ages of ages" do at first appear to say this, but this is not at all necessarily the meaning. In considering Mark 9:43-48 we say that the meaning there is that there will be a perpetual memorial of the righteous judgment of God, which will continue after it has achieved the destruction of the wicked. May not "the smoke of their torment" which "goeth up unto ages of ages: be just exactly this? When men were burned at the stake, the smoke of their torment would continue to rise long after the torment itself had ceased. So also we read in Revelation 19:3 that the smoke of the burning of "Babylon" goes up unto the ages of the ages. Whatever Babylon may be, the imagery here is of a burning city, and we know how the smoke of a burning city would continue to rise long after the last inhabitant had perished. May it not be that what can happen for some hours or days on earth is pictured here as happening through the ages of eternity? Evil shall be destroyed, God shall be all in all,[6] but the awful memorial of His righteous judgment and His final victory shall always remain as a testimony to angels and to men.

Revelation 20:10

"The devil that deceived them (the nations) was cast into the lake of fire and brimstone, where are also the beast and the false prophet; and they shall be tormented day and night unto the ages of the ages".

The word "are" is not in the Greek, and it is probably that instead of "are" should be supplied "had been cast"; see Revelation 19:20

---

[6] 1 Corinthians 15:28: see chapter 4.

where it is said that the Beast and the False Prophet were "cast alive into the lake of fire". But this makes no real difference to the sense, for in 20:10 it is said that "they", i.e., the Beast and the False Prophet as well as the Devil, shall be tormented for ever and ever. But between Revelation 19:20 and 20:10 "a thousand years had intervened (20:2, 7-10), no doubt a symbolic period, but surely representing a very long time. The lake of fire had held the Beast and the False Prophet for a thousand years, or whatever that symbol represents, without destroying them, and then after this they were to be tormented unto the ages of the ages.

But it is impossible in any case to build on this one verse the awful doctrine of the endless torment of all the lost, for the simple reason that it does not refer to human beings (or at any rate not to ordinary human beings) at all, but to the Devil, the Beast and the False Prophet. Many people understand the Beast and the False Prophet as institutions or abstractions, such as the apostate Christianity of Rome, or the anti-God spirit which is so prevalent in our own day. These interpretations would make this verse particularly difficult to understand. But even if the Beast and the False Prophet should be individual human beings, they are incarnations of Satan, filled with his spirit, and endowed by him with supernatural power (2 Thessalonians 2:8-10; Revelation 13:2,, 3, 11-15). Their fate, therefore, is no sort of indication of the fate of ordinary human beings.

It may be said that Matthew 25:41 shows that Human beings who go to hell will share the devil's fate. But the statement that they go "into the eternal fire prepared for the devil and his angels" does not at all necessarily mean that they remain alive in that fire as long as the devil would.

But does Revelation 20:10 really mean that the trinity of evil powers will be tormented *to all eternity*? There is a statement elsewhere which should make us pause before coming to a final conclusion in this matter. The strange prophecy about the King of Tyre in Ezekiel (28:11-19) contains a number of statements which could not apply to any human being, and the only being in the universe whom they would fit is Satan: see especially verses 13-

16. There is apparently a mingling of type and antitype here. The King of Tyre is denounced and threatened, but the prophet recognizes behind him a power mightier than he. Of this dread being, who was once "the anointed cherub that covereth" and was in Eden the garden of God, it is said "thou art become a terror, and thou shalt never be any more" (verse 19) . . . the same prophecy that had been applied to the city of Tyre in Ezekiel 27:36. We have seen that Paul's statement in 1 Corinthians 15:28 that God shall be all in all seems impossible to reconcile with the eternal existence of the devil, even in hell. Now in addition we have this definite statement in Ezekiel that the devil shall "never be any more", which seems to mean that his existence shall come to an end.

We must reconsider Revelation 20:10 in the light of these facts as well as of the general trend of Bible teaching on future punishment. It must be admitted that New Testament usage elsewhere is against interpreting "unto the ages of the ages" as meaning anything short of endless eternity. Outside the Book of Revelation it occurs seven times, always in ascriptions of praise to God, such as "to whom be glory for ever and ever". In Revelation itself it occurs twelve times: three times in ascriptions of praise: four times of God who "liveth for ever and ever" (4:9, 10; 10:6; 15:7); once of the reign of God and Christ (11:15); once of the reign of His saints (22:5); and in 14:11; 19:3 and the present verse in connection with judgment. But these facts however important are not finally conclusive. When this phrase is applied to the life of God or to the praise which His people will render to Him in eternity, it must mean for ever without end, because God Himself can never end, and He has given eternal life to His redeemed. But although the expression must mean a terribly long time, or what corresponds to such a thing in the timeless state, its meaning may well be limited to its contexts when it is applied to a being of whom it is said elsewhere that he is *not* absolutely eternal. If it be said that this is a juggling with words, we may reply that a legal document is not considered to be dishonest when it uses the term "in perpetuity" of an earthly transaction, although we all know that the world itself is not absolutely eternal.

In conclusion, we desire to disclaim dogmatic certainty on this tremendous question. It does seem to us that the general trend of

Bible teaching on future punishment points to destruction in the sense of the ending of conscious existence, though the process of destruction will involve penal suffering, which in certain cases, notably that of the Devil, may be awfully prolonged. And we believe that the explanations given above of the four apparent exceptions to the general teaching of Scripture are legitimate and consistent with reverence and honesty. But we acknowledge that, especially with regard to Revelation 20:10, there is a margin of uncertainty. All we can say is that, if the verse does really mean that absolutely endless torment will be the fate of the devil and the evil power inspired in him, a tremendous problem arises as to the eternity of evil, with regard to which we could only wait for further light till we know as we are known.

Additional Note to Chapter 5

The Unquenchable Fire

There is an explanation of the words "their fire is not quenched" (Isaiah 66:24, cp. Mark 9:48), which is different from that given above, but may possibly be the true meaning. Jeremiah wrote, "If ye will not hearken unto me . . . then will I kindle a fire . . . and it shall devour the palaces of Jerusalem, and it shall not be quenched" (Jeremiah 17:27). Jeremiah cannot have meant that Jerusalem would be destroyed by a fire that would burn for ever, for certainly this did not happen, and elsewhere Jeremiah looks forward to the restoration of God's people. He meant that the fire would burn until it had accomplished its purpose, no one would be able to put it out. It is possible then that the words in Isaiah "their worm shall not die, neither shall their fire be quenched" were meant in a similar sense. The worm would corrupt, and the fire would burn, until God's purposes were satisfied, but not necessarily for ever. If so, the same explanation would be valid in Mark.

This explanation is mentioned as showing how untrue it is that there is no honest alternative to everlasting torment as the explanation of Mark 9:43-48. But the present writer prefers the explanation given in chapter 3. It agrees better with Revelation 14:11 "The smoke of their torment goeth up forever and ever": also

Jeremiah 17:27 does not suggest any supernatural extension of the ordinary time required for fire to destroy a city, it merely says that the fire would not be quenched (till it had done its work). But in Isaiah it is otherwise: "From one new moon to another, and one sabbath to another, shall all flesh come to worship before me, saith Jehovah. And they shall go forth, and look upon the carcasses of the men that have transgressed against me: for their worm shall not die, neither shall their fire be quenched". The prophet evidently meant some supernatural extension of the time ordinarily required for burning dead bodies, and, as he was using the language of symbol, it seems more likely that an eternal memorial of God's wrath was meant (as in Revelation 14:11) than that the meaning should be, as in Jeremiah, that the fire should not be quenched till it had done its work.

Chapter 6: The Problem of Unequal Opportunity

The purpose of this chapter is to enquire what answer the Bible gives to a very important question. Does God make any distinctions in His judgments between those who have had little or no opportunity of accepting Christ, and those who have had the full light of the Gospel, but have rejected it? Even in Christian lands where the Gospel is preached, the opportunities of different individuals vary enormously. A child grows up in surroundings where the Name of God or Jesus Christ is never mentioned except in blasphemy. Neither in childhood nor in later life does it occur to him or to his associates to enter any place of worship, except perhaps for a wedding, a baptism, or a funeral. Though within reach of the Gospel, he never listens to it, and he lives without God and dies without Him. There are also villages, and even towns, where the pure Gospel is never preached by the regular ministers of the Churches; it is heard, if at all, only from travelling preachers. There are nominally Christian countries where much of the official priesthood of the so-called Christian Church is sunk in degrading superstition and sometimes even in vice. Is God going to deal with people, whose knowledge of the Gospel and opportunities of hearing it are so limited, in exactly the same way as He will deal with the child of a truly Christian home, or the member of a congregation which constantly hears the Gospel faithfully preached, if one who had such opportunities should reject the Lord Jesus Christ? In this chapter we are not concerned with our own or anyone else's ideas of what the answer to this question ought to be, but only to see what answer is given in the Word of God.

And beyond the problem of unequal opportunity in nominally Christian lands lies the further question of what will happen to those heathens and Moslems who have never heard the Gospel at all, at any rate so as to give them in God's sight a real opportunity of accepting it. It used to be believed that all of these, comprising the greater part of the human race, are inevitably doomed to hell. Has the Bible anything to say on this subject?

The Heathen Who Have Not Hear of Christ

We propose to consider first this latter problem, the case of those who have had *no* opportunity of accepting God's salvation offered through Christ, because they have never heard the Gospel at all. No clear revelation has been given to us on this matter, the main emphasis rests on our duty to bring the Gospel to them, and that is really what concerns us, rather than what God will do to those whom His people have failed to reach. But there are hints that they will be judged by a different standard from that which will be applied to those who have heard the Gospel.

"As many as have sinned without the law shall also perish without law: and as many as have sinned under law shall be judged by law . . . for when Gentiles which have no law do by nature the things of the law, these, having no law, are a law unto themselves; in that they shew the work of the law written in their hearts, their conscience bearing witness therewith, and their thoughts one with another accusing or else excusing them; in the day when God shall judge the secrets of men, according to my gospel, by Jesus Christ" (Romans 2:12, 14-16). These words do not suggest that ignorance of Christ will be in itself an adequate plea for acquittal at the Judgment, but that those who have not known Him will be judged according to the light which they had. It has been answered that in that case none of them would have any hope, because no one is able to live up to the light which he has, without the New Birth and the power of the Holy Spirit. But Paul, who was the last man to question this truth, clearly implies that some who were "without law" will be saved, and we may infer that there are mysteries in God's dealing with the heathen which have not been revealed to us. We are not entitled to use, with regard to them, arguments which would be perfectly valid with regard to those who have the light of the Gospel.

The Old Testament may help us to a little further understanding of this dark problem. The people of Sodom were not condemned for their failure to worship Jehovah, but for the wickedness of their lives. Jonah was not sent to rebuke the Ninevites for idolatry, but to summon them to repentance, because their wickedness had come up before Jehovah. (Jonah 1:2), and when they did repent, it was of their evil works and not, as far as we are told, of their worship of false gods (Jonah 3:8-10). The difference between the sins for which Judah and Israel on the one hand, and the heathen nations on the other, are condemned by Amos (chapters 1 and 2) is most instructive. Judah and Israel are denounced for offences against known commands of their God, the heathen nations for acts of outrageous cruelty. So also, in harmony with Amos' treatment of this matter, our Lord tells us that the final judgment of even such a city as Sodom would be "more tolerable" than that of those who had seen His mighty works but had not repented (Luke 10:12-14). He does not suggest that the people of Sodom would escape punishment, but He does say that their punishment would be less severe.

In general then, the judgment of God against heathen nations in the Old Testament is either for extreme offences against morality, which, it is implied, they knew to be wrong, or for attacks upon the people of Jehovah, which involved a deliberate defiance of their God.

Paul, in speaking of the times before Christ came, says that God "in the generations gone by suffered all the nations to walk in their own ways", and "the times of ignorance, therefore, God overlooked; but now he commandeth men that they should all everywhere repent" (Acts 14:16; 17:30). Yet Paul taught that the heathen were not wholly without responsibility, for God did not leave Himself without witness through His works (Acts 14:17; Romans 1:20). Paul finds the origin of heathenism in a deliberate rejection of a knowledge of God which all once had (Romans 1:20-23), and declares explicitly what the Old Testament seems to assume, that the fouler sins of heathenism are sins against the light which even the heathen have (Romans 1:32).

To sum up the matter. The little that is revealed to us about the judgment of the heathen seems to show that the Bible does not teach that those who die in heathen darkness without hearing the Gospel are all inevitably doomed to hell: but on the other hand it does not exempt them from all responsibility for their actions. God has His own special method of judging them, in accordance with the knowledge which they had, and the way they have used it.

It may be asked, how is it possible in any case for one who never accepted Christ to be saved? The Bible teaches vary plainly that there is no salvation in any other: "neither is there any other name under heaven, that is given among men, wherein we must be saved" (Acts 4:12). It is not necessary that we should be able to answer this question, for if God gives us an intimation that He has a different way of dealing with those who have not heard the Gospel, so that they are not all inevitably lost, then we can thankfully accept His word, and leave it to Him how He reconciles the forgiveness of their sin with His eternal justice. It is really His affair and not ours at all, and He tells us what we need to know, and not what does not concern us. But reverent conjecture may supply a provisional answer. One thing is surely certain. No one is saved by any other means than by the redeeming death of the Lord Jesus Christ on Calvary. But the redemption that is in Christ Jesus may, by God's special decree, be made available for people who have not rejected it, even though through ignorance they have not accepted it, provided that in His judgment they have obeyed the light which they had.

Some such theory seems necessary to cover the case of the little child who dies before he is old enough to be responsible in God's sight for the decision which determines eternal destiny. We do not know when that age is reached, it may differ from one child to another: God alone decides, and He has perfect knowledge of every case. We are perfectly sure that He who said "Suffer the little children to come unto me, for of such is the kingdom of heaven", would not send to hell little ones who had not reached the age of responsibility for the choice between right and wrong. But yet it must be through the Cross, and in no other way, that they too are saved, for the perverted nature which they have inherited would need to be cleansed by the Blood of Christ.

Degrees of Punishment

We have seen that the Bible does not teach that ignorance of the Gospel is itself enough to ensure salvation, and that though we have sufficient ground for hope that many who never heard the Gospel will be saved, there will alas also be many who will perish, because, like the people of Sodom and Gomorrah, they disobeyed the light which they had. But the question arises whether the punishment of such people who sinned grievously against the dim light of natural morality will be just the same as that of those who sinned against the full light of the Gospel. As has been pointed out already, our Lord has answered this question by comparing the case of Sodom and Gomorrah with that of those who had seen His mighty works, and rejected Him or refused to receive His disciples (Luke 10:12-14). This saying alone would be sufficient to establish the principle that there will be degrees of punishment in the next world

But it is not alone. As was remarked at the beginning of this chapter, there are great differences in the degree of opportunity and responsibility of people who are within reach of the Gospel. Our Lord has something to say about them too.

1. Mark 12:40. Here the official representative of religion is contrasted by implication with all others who have not his advantages, whether within or without the visible Church. The scribes "which devour widows' houses, and for a pretence make long prayers, these shall receive greater condemnation". The offenders have probably done no worse to the widows than an extortionate "publican" might do, but their guilt in God's sight is far deeper because of their much greater knowledge of His truth, and because they claimed to be His representatives and to be holy men. For this reason their punishment shall be more severe.

2. Luke 12:46-48. Here the distinction seems to be between varying degrees of unfaithfulness within the visible Church itself. First the true child of God, the faithful servant, is shown to us. The master of the house goes away, giving his steward charge over his household "to give them their

portion of food in due season". The faithful servant, whom on his return he finds so doing, will be set over all his master's property. Then our Lord deals with three cases of those who have the name but not the reality of being God's children. If the servant shamefully abuses his trust, "the lord of that servant shall come in a day when he expecteth not, and in an hour when he knoweth not, and shall cut him asunder, and appoint his portion with the unfaithful. And that servant which knew his lord's will and made not ready, nor did according to his will shall be beaten with many stripes: but he that knew not,[7] and did things worthy of stripes, shall be beaten with few stripes". The three types of unfaithful servants represent professing Christians, who in greater or lesser degree are false to their profession, and the cutting asunder and many and few stripes indicate different degrees of punishment.

It may be asked, Why only professing Christians? May not these verses speak of some kind of Purgatory, or even of punishment inflicted by God on His children in this life? The Roman Purgatory and punishments in this life are both outside the meaning of these verses, for in all our Lord's parables the Master's return always stands for His own Second Coming in judgment, so that the judgment referred to must be the Last Judgment. Morever the term "servant" is applied equally to the servant whose sentence is to be cut asunder, and whose portion is appointed with the unfaithful as to him who receives many or few stripes. The former judgment is obviously the extreme penalty of hell, so that the servant who receives it must be one who has made false profession of faith. But if "servant" can have that meaning in the one case, it can in the other two.

Others, who do not accept the Roman doctrine of Purgatory, assert that these verses indicate that hell itself may be a kind of Purgatory,

---

[7] If it be regarded as surprising that professing Christians should be represented as ignorant of their Lord's will, it may be replied that among professing Christians even today there is often appalling ignorance of the Bible and its teaching.

at least for most of those who go there, in which the soul is purified by disciplinary suffering, and ultimately restored. But it is a highly improbable explanation of these verses which would make them clash with the general witness of the New Testament that the judgment is final, and that there is no restoration. Nothing whatever is said in these verses to the effect that the servants might be restored to favour: that possibility simply is not mentioned. True, a flogging is not a sentence of death. But this is a parable, and the difference between degrees of the final punishment may well be represented by the difference between being cut asunder and a severe or mild flogging.

Nor is anything said about the duration of the penalty. But these verses agree very well with the conclusion which we have reached from the general teaching of the New Testament that the penal suffering of the lost is *not* endless. And this being so, degrees in the severity of the suffering would probably imply varying durations of it. But here we are in a region of speculation, for time itself is of this world. One thing is clear, that not all the condemned will suffer equally in the second death, and in view of the immense differences in opportunity and guilt among men, this conclusion is one which we may very thankfully accept.

A Second Chance After Death?

A theory which has found favour with many people is that after death another opportunity may be given for repentance and acceptance of Christ, to those who did not turn to Him in this life. We have seen already that the whole trend of Scripture teaching, and especially that of our Lord, is entirely opposed to any such opportunity being given after the Judgment. As Hebrews 6:2 says, it is an "eternal judgment", irreversible and final in its issue to all eternity.

But may there be an opportunity before the Judgment? Again the general sense of Scripture seems opposed to any such idea. "It is appointed unto men once to die, and after this cometh judgment" (Hebrews 9:27). "Behold, now is the acceptable time; behold now is the day of salvation" (2 Corinthians 6:2).

There is surely a good reason why the Bible is so silent on this subject. God wants to put all the emphasis on the absolute necessity of accepting Christ, and the certainty that those who refuse or neglect to accept Him will perish. The case of those who for no fault of their own have had no chance of hearing of Him is irrelevant to the main issue: and there ought not to be such people, it is a terrible approach to the Church of Christ that after 1900 years there are still so many who have never heard of His Gospel of salvation.

Finally, it must be said that though it may be very tempting to extend this theory to cover the case of those who had some opportunity, but what seems to us an inadequate one, of hearing the Gospel, we have no ground at all in Scripture for doing so. In all these difficult cases, we need to keep carefully to the plain teaching of the Bible that eternal life is only in Christ, and that this earthly life-time is the appointed time or opportunity: and then we must leave the "hard cases" to God, sure that whatever His decision is it will be absolutely just. It is He, not we, who will decide whether any soul really had a chance of deciding for Christ or not.

Chapter 7: Universalism

Universalism is the name given to the theory that although those who have rejected Christ will have to pass through a period of penal suffering in the next world, proportionate to their guilt, and to their obstinacy in refusing to turn to Him, all will eventually be saved. The foregoing pages will have shown that the whole body of Scripture teaching about future punishment is opposed to such a theory. Whether the words "death", "destruction", "perish", mean the end of existence or endless misery, in either case they signify a final doom. If "eternal punishment" is not an endless process of punishment, it is because it is a punishment with an endless result, a doom from which there is no return. And the terrible words which the Lord Jesus Himself spoke about the condemned all carry with them one dreadful implication of finality: for surely He would never have spoken so of any for whom He had hopes or purposes of redemption.

There are, however, certain texts which have been appealed to in support of the Universalist theory, and these must now be examined.

John wrote that Christ "is the propitiation for our sins; and not for ours only, but also for the whole world" (1 John 2:2).

Paul wrote that God "is the Saviour of all men, specially of them that believe" (1 Timothy 4:10); and that

God "willeth that all men should be saved, and come to the knowledge of the truth", and that

Christ "gave Himself a ransom for all" (1 Timothy 2:4, 6).

He also wrote that "the grace of God hath appeared, bringing salvation to all men" (Titus 2:11).

It is contended that the first two of these four texts assert plainly that the saving work of the Cross goes beyond those who believe, and covers the whole world: and that if, as the second two say, God wills that all men should be saved, and His grace brings salvation to all men, then none can finally perish.

But if this is the meaning of the words, it is very hard to reconcile it with the teaching of John and Paul elsewhere. John says that God "sent not the Son into the world to judge the world; but that the world should be saved through Him" (John 3:17). These words have some likeness to those of Paul that God willeth that all men should be saved, but they immediately follow the well-known words which say that God gave His only Son that "whosoever believeth on Him should not perish, but have eternal life". God's purpose in sending His Son was that the world should be saved through Him, but that purpose takes effect on those out of the world who believe on Him. And later in the same chapter we find, "He that believeth on the Son hath eternal life; but he that obeyeth not the Son shall not see life, but the wrath of God abideth on him" (John 3:36). Did John really mean that the words "shall not see life" were to be understood as "shall not see life, till he has suffered a temporary death", and that the wrath of God would "abide" till the condemned sinner should ultimately repent? Who could guess that the awful "lake of fire which is the second death" was really a "death" out of which would ultimately come repentance and restoration? Surely "death" would be a very ill-chosen word if such a thing were true, unless indeed something were said about "resurrection", but there is never any hint of resurrection from the second death.

Paul says that "the wages of sin is death; but the free gift of God is eternal life in Christ Jesus our Lord" (Romans 6:23): and he also said to Jews who had rejected the offer of salvation, "Your blood be upon your own heads" (Acts 18:6). These would be strange words to use, if the "death" were somehow going to end up in eternal life after all. When he speaks of those "that are perishing; because they received not the love of the truth, that they might be saved" (2 Thessalonians 2:10); or when he contrasts the "saved" and the "perishing", and describes their respective destinies as "death" and "life", it would be an extraordinary use of language, if behind the words lay the thought that those who "perished" would one day be saved, *after* they had perished. But above all, when he wrote of certain people that they were "the enemies of the cross of Christ: whose end is perdition" (Philippians 3:18, 19), that word "end" (to say nothing of "perdition") must have a very forced and unnatural sense, if the final destiny of those people is salvation. "End" can be a relative term when we are speaking of the end of earthly life, because we know that there is a life after earthly death: but Paul plainly means that the "end" of those people after earthly death is "perdition", and his words would be untrue if there could be a reversal of that "perdition" beyond the "end"!

The conclusion of all this is that the Universalist interpretation of these four texts which we have been considering can only stand, if it is clearly the only honest and natural explanation of them. But it is easy to show that this is by no means the case. In Ezekiel 18 it is asserted again and again that the wicked who persist in wickedness must die. But in the same chapter it is twice declared that God has no pleasure in the death of him that dieth, "Wherefore turn yourselves, and live" (verse 32: see also verse 23). Though God does not desire the death of the wicked, that does not save him if he does not turn and live: and there is no reason to suppose that Paul's words "God willeth that all men should be saved" meant anything inconsistent with the message of Ezekiel 18. It is instructive to compare 1 Timothy 2:6 "a ransom for all" with Mark 10:45 "a ransom for many". Paul's words mean literally "a substitute ransom on behalf of all": our Lord's words mean " a ransom instead of many". The substitute-ransom was offered on behalf of the whole world, but it was effectively "instead of" the "many" who accept it, and are saved by it. In Titus 2:11, the word rendered "bringing salvation" is the adjective "soterios", "saving", and the rendering "which has saving power for all men" would just as well express the sense. If we render "bringing salvation to all men", the words can very well mean "bringing the offer or power of salvation to all men", and this is the only explanation which agrees with Paul's teaching elsewhere.

The statement that God is the Saviour of all men (1 Timothy 4:10) could be most naturally made by anyone who believes in the message of John 3:16, without any though that He actually saves those who reject those who reject His salvation. There is no one, however hostile to God, to whom the question could not be addressed, "Will you really reject your Saviour?" But He is specially the Saviour of them that believe, for the words "your Saviour" have a far deeper meaning when addressed to the believer, whom God has actually saved, than when addressed to the unbeliever, whom God longs to save if he will turn to Him.

Thus these four texts simply express the universal love of God, and the universal offer of His salvation to those who persist in rejecting it.

"All Israel shall be saved . . . God hath shut up all unto disobedience, that He might have mercy upon all" (Romans 11:26, 32). Paul had explained that the greater number of the Jews has been removed from the blessings of God's covenant, on account of their rejection of the Gospel, and their place had been taken by the believing Gentiles. But, he adds, this is temporary only. God's rejection of Israel will only continue till "the fulness of the Gentiles" has come into His Church: then the Lord will come, and all Israel will turn to Him, and be saved. He adds that God in His wisdom has first used the fall of Israel as a means to the salvation of the Gentiles, and now He is using the salvation of the Gentiles as a means towards the salvation of Israel. It ought to be clear that Paul is not thinking of individuals but of groups, as in Ephesians 2. He does not mean that all the individual Jews who rejected Christ, and died in unbelief, would be saved: this would contradict his teaching elsewhere, and is not suggested by the argument here. He means that the Jewish *race* which had rejected Christ, and had been put out of the covenant for so doing, will one day accept Him, and be saved, not in part but wholly. But the individuals who will be saved will be those who compose "all Israel" at the time when it accepts Christ.

So also, the "all" who have been shut up unto disobedience means the human race, as divided into two groups, Jews and non-Jews. God has used each group as a means to the salvation of the other: but individuals in each group are only saved by personal faith in Christ during the time of opportunity. Compare Galatians 3:22, where this fact is made very clear. "Howbeit the scripture hath shut up all things under sin, that the promise by faith in Jesus Christ might be given to them that believe".

"As in Adam all die, so also in Christ shall all be made alive" (1 Corinthians 15:22). The very next verse explains what Paul meant by "all shall be made alive": "But each in his own order: Christ the firstfruit; then they that are Christ's at His coming". These words definitely limit the second "all" of verse 22 to those who are in Christ, even if that is not reasonably clear from verse 22 itself. In Adam all who are in him (that is, the whole human race) die (the death of the body): in Christ all who are in Him will be made alive (in the resurrection to life). There is another possible explanation by which the words "in Adam" are understood of unbelievers only in which case "die" must be understood of spiritual and eternal death, but this does not affect the explanation of the second half of the verse, with which we are concerned here.

"Every sin and blasphemy shall be forgiven unto men; but the blasphemy against the Spirit shall not be forgiven . . . whosoever shall speak against the Holy Spirit, it shall not be forgiven him neither in this world (age), nor in that which is to come" (Matthew 12:31, 32). On this passage the argument has been built that all sins except one shall be forgiven, if not in this age, then in what which is to come. But this is a distortion of our Lord's words. When He says that all sins shall be forgiven, of course He assumed that the necessary condition of repentance and faith is fulfilled. The one exception is an exception because in its own nature it makes repentance and faith impossible. But there is no suggestion in any of our Lord's words about judgment to come that repentance and faith will be possible in the world to come for those who have not repented in this world. So long as repentance and faith are possible, God would never finish with any soul. But the awful thing about our Lord's words of judgment is just this, that He implies so plainly that He *has* finished with those whom He condemns. He compares them to rubbish which men throw into the fire to be burned, because they have no use for it (Matthew 13:40-42, 47-50; John 15:6).

When, therefore, He says that sin against the Holy Spirit has no forgiveness in this world or in that which is to come, He is not implying that other sins will be forgiven in the world to come, He is simply intensifying the emphasis on the terrible statement that that sin has no forgiveness. It is the most emphatic way possible of saying "never".

"Whom (the Lord Jesus) the heaven must receive until the times of restoration of all things, whereof God spake by the mouth of His holy prophets which have been since the world began" (Acts 3:21). It is contended that "the restoration of all things" must include the restoration of the lost. But Peter is speaking here of something which he says was foretold by all the prophets, and also something connected with the Return of the Lord Jesus Christ. But the "restoration" to which the prophets looked forward was a setting up of right on the earth, the establishment of the Kingdom of God.

See for example Isaiah 1:26; 35; Jeremiah 33. Peter probably had in mind our Lord's sayings recorded in Matthew 17:11, "Elijah indeed cometh, and shall restore all things". See also Luke 1:17; Romans 8:21. The Greek in Matthew 17:11 has the verb from which the noun rendered "restoration" in Acts 3:21 is derived. In a certain sense, as our Lord went on to say, the prophecy had been fulfilled in John the Baptist: but it is generally agreed that His words do not exclude the idea that the full restoration or setting right is still to come, and is to be accomplished by the Lord Himself. The Millennial Kingdom is surely the final fulfilment of the prophecy. It seems then that Acts 3:21 cannot fairly be quoted as anything like a proof that there will be a universal salvation, including even those condemned at the Last Judgment. The most that can be said is that, if there were adequate evidence elsewhere that such a thing would take place, then Acts 3:21 might possibly include it, as the final conclusion of the restoration of which it speaks. But the restoration of the lost cannot possibly be the main and primary meaning of a restoration spoken of by all the prophets.

"Wherefore also God highly exalted Him, and gave unto Him the name which is above every name; that in the name of Jesus every knee should bow, of things in heaven and things on earth and things under the earth, and that every tongue should confess that Jesus Christ is Lord, to the glory of God the Father" (Philippians 2:9-11). It is contended that this is a statement that one day all without exception shall acknowledge Jesus as Lord, and therefore shall be saved. In chapter 5 (see pages above) this passage was quoted, and what we believe to be its true interpretation was summarily stated. The Universalists, however, do not acknowledge this interpretation legitimate, and it is necessary to give reasons for it here.

It should first be noted that these words are adapted from Isaiah 45:23, and are quoted more exactly in Romans 14:11. In Isaiah the context is an impassioned declaration that Jehovah alone is the true God. "There is no God else beside Me, a just God and a Saviour; there is none beside me. Look unto Me, and be ye saved, all the ends of the earth: for I am God and there is none else. By myself have I sworn . . . that unto Me every knee shall bow, every tongue shall swear" (Isaiah 45:21-23). What Isaiah is saying is that the day will come when all the world shall recognize Jehovah as the true God, and that there is none beside Him. He appeals to the ends of the earth to look to Jehovah and be saved, but he does not say that all will be saved. On the contrary, "all they that were incensed against Him shall be ashamed" (verse 24), a saying which is explained in Isaiah 41:11, "all they that are incensed against thee shall be ashamed and confounded: they that strive with thee shall be as nothing, and shall perish". Isaiah does not in any case say anything to suggest an ultimate turning to God of lost condemned sinners in the future state. His words most naturally suggest a universal homage to the One true God, without any necessary implication of a saving effect in all cases.

It must be granted, however, that New Testament quotations frequently develop and extend the meaning of the Old Testament original, which of course He who inspired both prophet and apostle had every right to do. Therefore after noting the meaning of the words in Isaiah, we must go on to examine the quotations in the New Testament.

- Romans 14:11 comes in a context where Paul is urging Christians not to judge one another in matters of eating and observing days. He says that none of us lives or dies to Himself. "For to this end Christ died, and lived again, that He might be the Lord of both the dead and the living". We are neither to judge nor to despise one another, "for we shall all stand before the judgment-seat of God. For it is written, as I live, saith the Lord, to Me every knee shall bow, and every tongue shall confess to God. So then each one of us shall give account to God" (see Romans 14:1-12).

Here it is plain that Paul is not thinking of the ultimate restoration of the condemned. On the contrary, he uses the quotation from Isaiah as proof that all Christians will appear before the judgment-seat of God.[8] How does he get that out of the prophet's words? He seems to understand "every knee shall bow" as a bowing in homage before the Judge, and the "confessing" would then be an acknowledgment of His holiness and justice. The idea of the worship which the redeemed offer to their Saviour God does not seem to be contemplated here, for this would hardly lead on to the thought of a judgment-seat. Then his thought seems to be that, since Isaiah's words apply to all, Christians must be included, therefore Christians too must give an account of themselves to God. Though details of this interpretation of Paul's thought may be questioned, it is surely clear that the idea of adoring worship, offered by those who have been condemned at the judgment and have been in hell, cannot possibly be fitted into these words.

- Philippians 2:9-11 is somewhat different from the Romans passage. Paul has been speaking of our Lord's wonderful humility in emptying Himself of His glory, that He might become man and die for man, and He went on to speak of how God had exalted Him, and given Him the name which is above every name. "that in the name of Jesus every knee should bow, of things in heaven and things on earth and things under the earth, and that every tongue should confess that Jesus Christ is Lord, to the glory of God the Father".

---

[8] The judgment of those for whom "there is no condemnation" (Romans 8:1) must of course be of a different kind from that of those who are not in Christ.

The main point here is the Divine glory of the ascended Lord. In Isaiah Jehovah had said, "By Myself have I sworn . . . unto Me every knee shall bow, every tongue shall swear". In Philippians it is the name of Jesus that every knee shall bow, and the confession of every tongue is to be that of Jesus Christ is Lord (where it seems probable that "Lord" stands for "Jehovah").

If then Paul is really saying that even the lost souls in hell will one day acknowledge Jesus as their Lord, and be saved, he is making this important revelation, so different from the general line of Bible teaching on the subject, quite by the way, in a sentence the main point of which is wholly different. Is this likely? Moreover, it should be noticed that he does not say "*their* Lord", and that there is no mention of salvation.

We turn back to Romans 14, remembering how there Paul connects the words "to Me every knee shall bow" with the judgment, and understands them as meaning the homage paid to the Judge. Here in Philippians his interpretation of the same Old Testament passage is not likely to be wholly different. The main thought is the Divine glory of the Lord Jesus: Paul says that every created intelligence in heaven, in earth and under the earth which may quite possible mean in hell) shall bow before the glory in homage, and every tongue shall confess that Jesus is Jehovah, to the glory of God the Father. But not a word is said as to the saving effect of this homage.

There is one other passage which, though it is not based on Isaiah 45:23, is very like Philippians 2:9-11, especially in the fact that its main point is the Divine glory of the Lord Jesus. In Revelation 5:12, the Seer tells of how he hears the angels and the redeemed in heaven ascribing glory to the Lamb, and then in the next verse he says, "And every created thing which is in heaven, and on the earth, and under the earth, and on the sea, and all things that are in them, heard I saying, Unto Him that sitteth on the throne, and unto the Lamb, be the blessing and the honour and the glory and the dominion, for ever and ever". It seems to us strange that this verse should be taken as a support for the Universalist position. Surely verse 12 describes the worship offered by angels and redeemed men, while verse 13 poetically depicts Nature as joining in the song of praise. "Every created thing which is in the heaven, and on the earth, and under the earth, and on the sea, and all things that are in them": these words plainly suggest the non-human creation. If it be said that mankind must be included in "every created thing", we would reply that the salvation of all mankind without exception cannot possibly be described in the 5th chapter of Revelation, before the great drama of the temporary triumph and final downfall of wickedness on earth has been displayed to the Seer. It would be very badly out of place. If such a thing as the ultimate salvation of the condemned were indeed described in Revelation, its place would surely be in the 22nd chapter, after the Judgment of the Great White Throne, and the creation of the new heaven and earth. But we look in vain for anything of the kind there.

Returning to the other three passages (Isaiah 45:23; Romans 14:11; Philippians 2:9-11), definite reasons have been given for the view that the leading thought is the recognition of God's glory and the offering of homage to Him, without any necessary implication of a saving effect. It will be part of the punishment of those who have ignored and resisted God in this life, to be compelled to acknowledge His divine glory, and offer Him unwilling homage. Not one of the three passages, considered with its context, suggests any idea of the ultimate salvation of those who have died without Christ.

In conclusion, we have seen that none of the texts which we have examined can rightly be used to prove the Universalist theory, when the context of the passages themselves and the teaching of the writers of them elsewhere are taken into account, and that the whole tenor of Scripture teaching about the last things is against Universalism. This theory requires a strange double use of the word "saved", and a most unnatural use of the words "perish" and "death". In any place where those who are "saved" are contrasted with those who "perish", the Universalist must agree with us that "saved" means "saved from perishing". The "saved" in this sense are those who accept the Lord Jesus in this life, and do not perish. But he interprets the words "perish" and "death" as meaning a ruin which is not irretrievable, but will end in ultimate repentance and salvation. And in certain special texts he asserts that the word "saved" can mean not "saved *from* perishing", but "saved *after* perishing". We claim that these interpretations are contrary to the natural use of language, and that there is nothing in the Bible to justify them. Salvation is salvation, offered here and now, to be accepted now, and delivering the soul from death, and there is no other salvation than this. Therefore those who do not receive this salvation must perish, and it is as true that those who perish are never saved, as it is that those who are saved never perish.

Chapter 8: Conclusions Summarized

The purpose of the present chapter is to summarize the conclusions reached in the foregoing chapters, and to consider the doctrine as a whole.

An enquiry into the meaning of the word "eternal" showed that, though permanence is an essential part of it, this does not necessarily prove that eternal punishment must be a punishment which the condemned endure in a conscious existence for ever and ever. The Bible speaks of "eternal salvation", "eternal judgment", "an eternal sin" (Hebrews 5:9; 6:2; Mark 3:29 R.V.). But these expressions do not mean a salvation which is eternally being affected, or a judgment which is eternally being pronounced, or a sin which is eternally repeated: they mean a salvation, a judgment and a sin which have eternal results. So then just as we are saved for ever, we are not for ever being saved, so we believe that the term "eternal punishment" does not mean that the condemned will for ever be in a state of being punished, but rather that they will be punished for ever, i.e., that they will be for ever separated from God and their existence will be ended for ever. At least we believe that the words can mean this; whether they do, depends on the general teaching of the Bible on the doom of the condemned.

But apart from four or five passages, there is not even an appearance of teaching everlasting torment in the Bible. What it does teach is that He who had said "Come unto Me, all ye that labour and are heavy laden", and "Him that cometh to Me I will in no wise cast out", will say to those whom He condemns, "Depart from Me, all ye workers of iniquity",[9] and they will be driven into the outer darkness, separated by an eternal judgment from God's presence. The Lord Jesus and John the Baptist compare them to useless weeds or chaff, thrown into the fire to be burned up, or again to barren branches of the vine, which men gather, and cast

---

[9] Matthew 11:28; John 6:37; Luke 13:28.

them into the fire and they are burned. It will be observed that it is the destructive function of fire which is emphasized here, but of course destruction by fire is a very awful thing, and it is made clear that there will be penal suffering, and in that furnace of fire there will be "weeping and gnashing of teeth". Again, our Lord compares man's killing of the faithful disciple with God's punishment of the apostate, and says that man can kill the body but not the soul, but God can destroy both soul and body in hell.[10]

Throughout the Acts and the Epistles the doom of the condemned is spoken of as death or destruction: Paul repeatedly refers to those without Christ as "they that are perishing", in the Epistle to the Hebrews we read of "a fierceness of fire that shall devour the adversaries", and in the Book of Revelation the lake of fire is defined as "the second death".[11] Nowhere in Acts or Epistles is anything said to suggest that these words are not to be understood in their plain meaning. On the contrary, a comparison of 1 Timothy 6:16 with Romans 6:23 and similar statements elsewhere plainly implies that "death" should be understood as the end of existence where the ultimate result of sin is spoken of. God only has immortality, and eternal life is His gift, bestowed on the believer through Jesus Christ, but the wages of sin is death. Thus the general drift of the teaching both of our Lord and His apostles about future punishment is that it will be a final exclusion from God's presence, a destruction for ever (Psalm 92:7), from which there can be no return. The Bible nowhere gives any ground for hope that any who have been condemned will ever be restored to eternal life with God. The judgment, the punishment, the destruction are eternal.[12] The destruction moreover will be by "fire", which must involve awful suffering, "weeping and gnashing of teeth". But it should be added here that there is plain evidence in our Lord's words that there will be degrees of severity in this terrible punishment, proportioned to the knowledge of and responsibility of the condemned.[13] The

---

[10] Matthew 3:12; 13:40-42; John 15:6; Matthew 10:28.
[11] 1 Corinthians 1:18; 2 Corinthians 2:18; 4:3; 2 Thessalonians 2:10; Hebrews 10:27; Revelation 20:14; 21:8.
[12] Hebrews 6:2; Matthew 25:46; 2 Thessalonians 1:9.
[13] Mark 12:40; Luke 10:12, 14:12:46-48

problem of how God will deal with those who had no opportunity at all in this present life is another matter, on which the Bible gives us dim hints rather than plain teaching (see chapter 6 above). For the main concern of Divine Revelation is to impress on those who do hear the Gospel message the urgency of accepting, and the awful consequence of rejecting it.

We have seen that this is the bearing of all references to future punishment in the New Testament with the apparent exception of four or five passages, and we have examined the seeming exceptions. The true force of Matthew 18:34, 35 (like Matthew 25:41, 46) is to emphasize the finality of the judgment, and close the door to any hope of restoration. Sin is compared to an unpayable debt: a slave handed over to the tormentors till he should pay two million pounds would never come out free, and would suffer awful things, but in the end he would assuredly die. In Mark 9:43-48 our Lord compares the doom of the lost to the destruction of corpses by a worm that never dies and a fire that is never quenched. The comparison of these words with Isaiah 66:24 from which they are quoted suggests that what He meant was not an endless existence in torment (for corpses do not suffer) but rather a perpetual memorial of God's righteous judgment which will for ever remain after all evil has been destroyed. This same memorial of judgment seems to be referred to in the words "the smoke of their torment goeth up for ever and ever" (Revelation 14:11). Long after death had ended the sufferings of a man burned at the stake, the smoke of his torment would continue to rise: and what can happen for some hours on earth is pictured here as happening through the ages of eternity.

- Revelation 20:10 refers only to the Devil and the two evil powers energized by him. It therefore cannot by itself teach the everlasting torment of ordinary human beings in hell. Whether it intends to teach the everlasting torment of the trinity of evil of whom it speaks, is a very difficult question. It certainly appears to do so, but consider again (the previous section 'Revelation 20:10') which provide strong reasons have been given for questioning whether in this particular case the phrase "for ever and ever" (Greek, to the ages of the ages) has the absolute meaning "to all eternity" which it seems to have elsewhere in the New Testament.

General Remarks on the Doctrine

It is impossible even to begin to understand eternal punishment, if it is considered in isolation from the Problem of Evil and the Doctrine of the Atonement. Why evil was allowed to come into the universe is an insoluble mystery: but it is certainly here, and it is certain that a holy God cannot have fellowship with it, and must will its destruction. But because God is Love, He longs to save man from destruction, and the Bible tells us that through the Cross He found a way of condemning sin and yet saving the sinner, a way infinitely costly to Himself. But the purpose of that Sacrifice was not only to save the sinner from death, but also to save him from sin. The sinner must repent – that is, he must desire to be delivered from sin – and he must believe in his Saviour. Those who refuse God's salvation on God's conditions are not saved by the sacrifice of the Cross, they come before His judgment with their sin, and the wages of sin is death.

What is ultimately to happen to the evil which has defiled God's creation? God provided a way of redemption, and thereby many of His sin-defiled creatures have been and are being separated from their sin, and He has given to them eternal life that they may be with Him for ever. But for those who choose evil, and reject God's way of deliverance from it, there is nothing left but to share the doom of that evil principle which they have made their own. It must be destroyed when the kingdom of God becomes supreme, for evil cannot be permanent in the universe, and as they have refused the only way of becoming separated from it, they must be destroyed with it. This the thought which is expressed by the Lord Jesus Himself, when He says that He will tell the condemned to go into the eternal fire prepared for the devil and his angels. The destruction must be eternal – that is, final – for evil can only be destroyed it cannot be reconciled with good.[14] The one and only way of reconciling the sinner to the holy God, by separating him from his sin, has in their case alas been rejected, and there remains no other sacrifice for sin.

This we believe to be the fundamental principle of eternal punishment, that evil must ultimately be destroyed out of God's universe, and that the sinner who rejects God's way of salvation, whereby he might be separated from his sin, must perish. This is primary and fundamental: all else, even the awful fact of penal suffering in the process of destruction, is secondary.

The Awfulness of the Second Death

But let none imagine that because eternal punishment does not mean everlasting torment, therefore it is a mild penalty which need not be dreaded. There are some who would rather welcome the idea of no life after death, and who might imagine that a penalty which ends at last in the cessation of existence would not be so very terrible. No more dreadful mistake could be made than so to consider the matter. The annihilation of the lost, as we believe it is taught in the New Testament, must not be confused with the unbeliever's notion of no life after (bodily) death. The soul which goes out into the dark without Christ does not cease to exist *then*. It must await the Day of Judgment. But before the Judgment will come the "resurrection to judgment" (John 5:29; Revelation 20:11-15). Then the personality will be completed by the reuniting of soul and body, not for the joy of fellowship with God, but for the suffering of the final doom. Having face death once in this world, the lost soul must face it again, under circumstances of unutterable shame and horror. God will not then be One who can be ignored or patronized, He will be known for what He is, the One who fills heaven and earth. Then the Almighty King, who had offered him

---

[14] The Bible declares that the present mixture of good and evil in the world will not be tolerated for ever. God will one day take to Himself the kingdom and good will finally triumph. Then, not only in the world but in the whole created universe, God will be all in all. See, e.g., Revelation 11:15; 19:6; 21:1-5; 1 Corinthians 15:28.

salvation and would so gladly have saved him, will reject him and pronounce him only fit for destruction.

The instinct, which so often makes even the suicide struggle desperately for life at the last, will surely be far more powerful as the soul faces the final disintegration of personality, the utter end, and what an awful end! How terrible the process of destruction will be will depend on the degree of each soul's guilt before God, how much opportunity has been enjoyed, how much light has been disobeyed. But in any case what an awful thing it must be to be rejected by God as worthless, and cast upon the bonfire as rubbish to be destroyed, realizing as never before what might have been if God's salvation had been accepted. Remember those words of the Lord Jesus Christ, which He uttered in His loving desire to save men from that awful doom. "There shall be weeping and gnashing of teeth, when ye shall see Abraham, and Isaac, and Jacob, and all the prophets in the kingdom of God, and yourselves cast forth without" (Luke 13:28).

May we take warning while there is yet time.

The Righteous Judge

Part 2

Objections Answered

Introductory Remarks

The doctrine stated in the foregoing chapters is open to attack from two sides. To some it will seem to be a dangerous compromise with unbelief, convinced as they are that the traditional doctrine of Everlasting Torment has the full authority of Scripture. To others, however, it may seem open to a number of objections from the opposite standpoint, namely that the severity it attributes to God is incompatible with His character.

The present writer, as far as his own thinking goes, feels that the only question that really matters is whether or not he has rightly interpreted the Word of God. Only God knows the facts, and if His revelation of them is rightly interpreted, no tradition (even an evangelical tradition) has a good claim to be heard against it: and, on the other hand, quarrelling with facts does not change them.

In the following chapters an attempt will be made to meet the objections raised by those who do not see the matter in the same light.

Chapter 9: Objections from the Traditional Side

Many who accept the authority of the Word of God will object that in this matter of eternal punishment we have deserted the old paths and gone astray into strange doctrine. Now the old paths are good, very good, when they are Bible paths, and it is far from our desire to desert them. But we Evangelicals, who criticize the Roman Church for putting tradition on a level with the Bible, must be very careful that we ourselves do not unwittingly fall into the same snare. Every Evangelical, we are sure, would agree in theory with this proposition: but the mind naturally tends to be suspicious of an interpretation of Scripture which clashes with a traditional belief held by saintly men of God for centuries past.

Nevertheless, we appeal to those who hold the traditional view to accept our solemn assurance that in intention at least we are as loyal to the Word of God as they are, and on that basis to give a fair consideration to the explanations of it which we have put forward. For it is on Scriptural grounds, and no other, that we have abandoned the traditional theory. It may have been noticed that in the foregoing chapters, though the traditional view was rejected, there was no denunciation of it on the ground that it is a dreadful libel on the character of God to say that He would condemn any of His creatures to everlasting torment. This is not because we do not recognize that there is here a very real and terrible difficulty in the traditional view, for we are sure that all who hold that view, and have reflected on its meaning, are intensely conscious of the difficulty, and would not believe in everlasting torment, but that they are convinced that faithfulness to the Word of God compels them. But we feel unable to regard this difficulty as fundamental, or as in itself a sufficient reason for rejecting the traditional doctrine. For the words of the Lord Jesus Christ with regard to the condemned are so terrible, so final in excluding any idea that mercy may be open to them, that we dare not presume to set limits in advance as to what He might see fit to ordain as their punishment. The character of God is safe in the hands of His Son, who came to reveal Him, and we must trust Him, and receive what He tells us. The question is simply, *What do His words mean?*

But the fundamental reasons which led the present writer to abandon the doctrine of everlasting torment are two, both founded on the Word of God itself.

1. First, the Bible teaching that God will sum up all things in Christ, and that ultimately He Himself will be all in all, seems incompatible with the eternal existence of sin and sinners in hell.
2. Secondly, the belief that the Bible teaches everlasting torment rest mainly upon the notion that every soul, good or evil, is immortal; and this latter idea is entirely lacking in Bible authority.

We grant that, if it be assumed that no soul can die the whole body of New Testament teaching on future punishment is unanimous that it will be everlasting misery. For if the soul cannot die, "death" and "destruction" as applied to it must mean a wretched existence, and this can never end, for the New Testament is very clear that there is no escape from perdition into everlasting life. So also "eternal punishment" would necessarily mean a punishment endlessly suffered, for the whole usage of the word "eternal" forbids the idea of a punishment from which the soul could escape and live. But put on one side that traditional belief that every soul must be immortal, and the immense majority of Bible texts about the doom of the condemned are seen to teach their destruction, not their endless torment. In our Lord's teaching, even the two or three texts which have some appearance of teaching everlasting torment, have that appearance mainly because of the unconscious influence of that traditional but unscriptural belief. Why else should it be taken for granted that the undying worm and the unquenchable fire of Mark 9:43-48 will be everlastingly tormenting the living souls and bodies of the lost, when Isaiah, whom our Lord was quoting, wrote of corpses?

But what of Revelation 20:10 "they (the devil, the beast and the false prophet) shall be tormented for ever and ever"? Well, if it be assumed that no soul can die, then Revelation 20:10 is merely an exceptionally clear statement of a doom which has been pronounced upon all the lost by the whole body of New Testament teaching. Remove that assumption, and Revelation 20:10 is a very perplexing apparent exception to the main trend of the New Testament teaching, and as such we have discussed it above. In any case, as we have pointed out, it refers only to the three supreme powers of evil.

But it may be objected that the abandonment of the doctrine of everlasting torment blunts the weapon of the Gospel, and weakens its appeal. We are sure that those who use this argument would at once agree that no supposed effects of a doctrine would justify us in accepting or clinging to it, if it is not taught in the Word of God. They might argue, however, that this bad effect of abandoning the doctrine creates a strong presumption that something is wrong with the interpretation of Scripture which we have set out above. We still claim that ultimately the only question is, what does the Bible really say? But the fear of a bad effect on the Gospel message seems to us to be completely mistaken. Whatever may have been the case in the past, in these days the doctrine of everlasting torment drives the unsaved further away from God, not to Him. And in practice it is very rare indeed that this doctrine, *clearly stated* is made the instrument of an evangelistic appeal. We agree heartily that any suggestion that somehow all will come right in the end does grievously blunt the Gospel message. But the doctrine that the condemned will perish by an awful death, finally excluded from God's presence, has nothing in common with such a suggestion. The choice is still between eternal life with God and an awful death in the outer darkness.

But is not the belief that the unsaved are going into an eternity of endless torment the mightiest motive for soul-winning? Again we would say, Search the Scriptures. Examine every text from which the duty of witnessing for Christ or leading others to Him can be inferred, and see if you can find one which connects soul-winning with even a seeming suggestion of the doctrine of endless torment. Paul was a mighty soul-winner. But, if the driving force of his evangelism had been that doctrine, could he have kept silence about it or hinted distantly at it? He would never have been content to use words like "them that perish" or "destruction", he would have made clear that the awful thought of the everlasting torment of the unsaved was ever pressing upon him. It is plain that he was in fact powerfully influenced by the desire to save men from perishing (see e.g., Acts 20:26): but for that very reason it seems to us incredible that, if he had thought of their doom as everlasting torment, he should always have used words about it which in themselves fall far short of suggesting such a thing. Paul was not accustomed to hint at things about which he felt strongly. If then the endless torment of the lost are never mentioned in Scripture as a motive for soul-winning, they cannot be essential for that purpose.

In conclusion we would appeal to those who accept the doctrine of everlasting torment to consider very carefully whether, quite unconsciously, their belief has been resting more on tradition than on the Word of God. By "tradition" we mean first the traditional interpretation of two sayings of our Lord, and two verses in Revelation; and secondly the even more potent, but perhaps unrecognized, influence of the traditional belief that no soul can ever die. No Protestant should object to being asked to re-examine any traditional belief in the light of the Word of God, searching the Scriptures to see whether these things be so.

Chapter 10: Why Should This Life Be Decisive?

The objections now to be considered are of a very different type from those discussed in the last chapter: they are raised by people who would regard the doctrine set out in the first nine chapters as preferable to the traditional doctrine of everlasting torment, but nevertheless, too severe to be compatible with the nature of God as revealed to us in Christ.

For instance, why should this short life be sufficient to decide the eternal destiny of a soul? Although this difficulty is greatly diminished by the abandonment of the doctrine of everlasting torment, it is by no means removed. The eternal extinction of a soul is a very awful thing to be dependent on a few short years of life in this world. It has been admitted in Chapter 6 that there are great differences in the degree of opportunity of accepting Christ, which is given to different people. In one extreme case, that of those who have never heard of Him, the possibility has been admitted that they may be given an opportunity in the life beyond the grave, and that their destiny may be decided by the use which they make of this opportunity. Why not extend this principle to its logical conclusion, that all who have not rejected Christ with the fullest knowledge of what they were doing should have a time of discipline and probation in the world to come, during which they would have a full opportunity of understanding the Gospel and accepting it?

There are here two problems, which though they are connected are distinct, and should be considered separately:

1. First, the problem of unequal opportunity, and
2. Secondly, the question whether the present life is long enough to provide an adequate basis for an eternal judgment by the righteous God.

Unequal Opportunity

In Chapter 6 an attempt was made to discover what the Bible has to say on this subject. It is necessary now to re-examine the conclusions there reached in the light of the objections of those who would not be satisfied to accept Bible authority as conclusive. We saw that there are several indications in the New Testament that there will be degrees of punishment in the next world corresponding to the degree of guilt of the condemned. But eternal life is in Christ, and in Christ alone: a man passes into the next world either in Christ or without Him, and if without Him, he cannot have eternal life which is "the gift of God through Jesus Christ our Lord". In Chapter 6 we considered the case of those who have no opportunity at all of accepting Christ, who therefore cannot be judged to have either rejected or ignored Him. In their case there are hints in the Bible that God will deal with them in some special way, and we venture to express the opinion that they may have an opportunity of making their choice after death. But this provisional statement of opinion cannot justly be used as a "thin end of the wedge" to force us to admit the theory of a second chance after death for those who have heard the Gospel, or could have heard it if they would.

It is indeed quite possible that there may be people in nominally Christian countries, especially in those where official Christianity preaches a false Gospel, who may be adjudged by God Himself to have had no real opportunity of knowing the Gospel of salvation. If so, we may presume that He would deal with them as He deals with the heathen, which is what they really are. In all difficult questions of apparently inadequate opportunity we must remember that the Judge is omniscient as well as perfectly just, and He, not we, will decide whether any individual has or has not had a real opportunity of accepting Christ. But we need to remember also that He has made it plain that neglect of opportunity is much the same in His sight as rejection (Hebrews 2:3; Matthew 12:30). We repeat then that the Bible doctrine is that eternal life is in Christ alone, and those who will be adjudged by God to have either ignored or rejected Him will not receive that gift, and therefore must "perish". It follows that degrees of penalty cannot affect the issue of life or death, but concern penal suffering which accompanies the death penalty.

"Is this credible"? says the objector, "Why should the justice of God know only one penalty, capital punishment, varied only by the degrees of accompanying suffering? What should we say of a human penal code based on such a principle?" Of course it is not true that God's justice knows only the death penalty. During the present life He, like the enlightened human judge, does frequently punish with a view to reformation. He inflicts the death penalty when the time for reformation has gone by. But in any case there are important differences between an earthly judge and God. The earthly judge represents the interests of the community, to which he and the offender both belong. Punishments inflicted by him ought to protect the community, while at the same time, as far as possible, the hope of correcting and reforming the offender is kept in view. And if he does sentence an offender to death, he takes from him life which neither he, nor the community in whose name he acts, had given. God, however, is not one of the community of men acting on behalf of the whole. He is the Creator and Sovereign Lord of all men, whom He framed for Himself, and the life and soul and body which they possess is His gift. Has He not every right to make the eternal continuance of that gift conditional on obedience to His righteous laws? Moreover God so loved the world, that He gave His only begotten Son, that whosoever believeth on Him should not perish, but have eternal life. In view of this, has not God still more the right to say that eternal life shall be in His Son alone, and that those who neglect or reject Him shall not receive it?

The Shortness of This Life

But the question still remains, is not this life too short to decide the issues of eternity? We may ask in reply, what would be long enough, if the matter be considered in terms of time? Suppose God were to grant an extension of the day of grace far into the next life, there must needs be an end to it sometime, and, whenever the end came, the time of probation would still be as nothing in comparison with eternity. But in spiritual matters it is not quantity but quality which counts.

It has been shown in Chapter 6 that the Bible puts the close of the present life as the furthest limit of the time of opportunity. But indeed the present life is the time within which the opportunity comes, but the actual decisive moment, on which the issues of eternity really depend, is not the whole span of the present life or anything like it. It may be a year, or a month, or a week; it may even be one day, or one hour.

There are those who hear the Gospel often, and only grow harder in their resistance to its claims, and as far as can be known this resistance continues to the end. But again and again it has been found in such cases that there has been a time, perhaps in youth, when there was for a while an inclination towards Christ, when the heart was moved and impressed and almost ready to yield. But the decision was made to reject or postpone the answer, and the desire for Christ died and never revived again.

Let there be no misunderstanding here. It is not suggested for one moment that any living human being who turn to God in true desire for His salvation in Christ would be rejected, however much he had spurned His gracious offer before. "Him that cometh to Me I will in no wise cast out" (John 6:37). But the awful danger of spurning the offer of grace is just this, that the offer may not be repeated, and unless the Holy Spirit speaks to a soul, there can be no desire for God, no turning to Him in repentance and faith. This is the tremendous force of the words, "Now is the acceptable time, now is the day of salvation", for he who rejects or postpones acceptance of Christ cannot know whether he is rejecting his last chance. God has said "Now", and though there may be another opportunity, there is no promise that there will be.

Experience has proved again and again that, however many may be the minor crises in a spiritual life, there is a supreme hour of decision on which everything depends, and that hour is not usually very long in terms of time. Even in the case of those whose contact with the Gospel is apparently almost nil, who never go to a place of worship, and seem to pass their whole lives in complete indifference to God, there must often be occasions when the claims of Christ come before them, if not directly, then at least indirectly through its being brought to their notice that within their reach there are places where they may hear about Him. We believe than in most cases, perhaps all, there is some occasion when an impulse to move in His direction presents itself, either from within or as a suggestion from someone else, and is rejected or deferred to some other time which does not come. Such occasions may be rare in any individual case, but their very rarity is just our present point, which is that this life is not itself the time of opportunity, but the time within which the opportunity presents itself.

This being so, nothing would be gained if the time within which salvation may be accepted were to be extended still further. For if the present life is only the outer circle within which the point of the decisive hour is included, to widen the circle would not enlarge the point. But it may be said that there is a fallacy here, for we are taking no account of the great difference in the conditions of the life to come, when the soul will have discovered the realities of eternity: would not that make all the difference? It is difficult to discuss what may happen in conditions of which we have no experience, when revelation is not allowed a decisive voice. But this may be said with regard to what the Bible tells us, that there is never any statement that in the next life people *repent*, and are then told that it is too late. Unavailing regret might be possible, but not a change of attitude towards God. But even if repentance be not in itself impossible after death, as we believe, it should be pointed out that the entry into the eternal state would not in itself be likely to make for repentance. It would assuredly bring a devastating discovery of the worthlessness of earthly things in comparison with eternal things. But would such a discovery tend to produce a true repentance? We may perhaps find an analogy in the effect which contact with the supernatural produces on people in this life. It does not by any means necessarily lead to repentance. The Pharisees saw our Lord's miracles, but instead of repenting they sought for a way of avoiding the necessity of confessing that they had been wrong in rejecting Him, and found it in attributing His power to the devil!

So then our reply to the objection that this short life ought not to be decisive for eternity may be summed up thus. As far as this life is concerned, the evidence of experience confirms the Bible teaching that the decisive hour is short, and that means that there would be no gain in extending the time within which that decisive hour might come. In any case, any finite period is as nothing relative to eternity. And there is no good reason to suppose that the changed conditions of the next life would make decision for Christ more likely in the cases of those who had not accepted Him here.

Chapter 11: Objections to the Extinction of Existence

Many people feel that there is something outrageous and monstrous about a theory that, in certain circumstances, human existence can come to an end. "It is intelligible that unbelieving materialists should talk about man 'going out like a candle', but it is strange indeed that a Christian should admit such a possibility even for the worst of men! It is one of the great merits of Christianity that it bears witness to the eternal value of the human soul, and declares that man's strong instinct that he is not going to perish is a true instinct implanted by God. It is an outrage against the dignity of humanity to suggest that any human personality can come to an end."

The strength of these objections is partly derived from the belief, by no means limited to Christians, that the immortality of every soul is a fundamental teaching of Christianity. The Christian who questions it seems therefore to be straying from the Christian position, and linking himself with the materialist.

We have shown in Chapter 1 that universal immortality is not taught in Scripture, and therefore cannot be a fundamental of the faith. But, apart from this, it is not difficult to show that our position is essentially different from that of the materialist. He believes in no life after death for anyone, because he disbelieves in God, and regards human life as merely a physical property of the human body, which perishes with it.

We believe, however, that human life, whether in this world or the next, is the gift of God. We believe also that God-given life is not ended by bodily death, but that if a man is in Christ he has life eternal in Him, and if he is not in Christ his life continues until God's judgment ends it. Nothing could be more fundamentally different from materialism than this.

But our objector says that it is one of the great merits of Christianity that it bears witness to the eternal value of the human soul, and he goes on to speak of the "dignity of humanity". There is confusion of thought here. Assuredly Christianity does witness to the value of eternal things as compared with temporal. Our Lord certainly said "What doth it profit a man to gain the whole world, and forfeit his life (or, soul)?" (Mark 8:36). But it is no part of the message of Christianity to emphasize the dignity of *humanity in revolt against God*. It was not because of His sense of the dignity of humanity, but because of His love for it in its lost ruined state, that God gave His only Son to die for it. See, e.g., John 3:16; Luke 19:10. So then in answer to the complaint that the extinction of a human soul would be contrary to the dignity of human personality, we reply that the "lost" and the "perishing" have no dignity but only need, and that their only hope is to recognize their need and humbly to accept God's offer of salvation.

And the argument from human instinct is wrongly stated. Although it is necessary to be careful not to assume too quickly that a widespread human belief is a God-implanted instinct, we believe that there really is an instinctive feeling among men that death of the body is not the end of existence. As Tennyson wrote,[15]

> "Man thinks he was not made to die,
> And Thou hast made him, Thou art just."

Such an instinct most probably is from God, for it is fully corroborated by the Scriptures, and it may even have originated in God's revelation of Himself to man at the beginning, but we doubt very much whether this instinctive feeling goes beyond a belief in our survival of bodily death. To assert that the new existence beyond the grave, of which none of us have any experience, is necessarily endless, is quite another matter, and no human instinct could prove such a thing.

If it be said, however, that the theory of conditional immortality means that man *was* made to die ultimately, but that God gives

---

[15] *In Memoriam.*

immortality to some men … we would disagree with that statement as God made man for Himself, and therefore for life not death. Man, however, chose to disobey God, and with disobedience came death.

> "In that day that thou eatest thereof thou shalt surely die" (Genesis 2:17).

> "The soul that sinneth, it shall die" Ezekiel 18:4).

> "Through one man sin entered into the world, and death through sin; and so death passed unto all men, for that all sinned" (Romans 5:12).

From Paul's language elsewhere (e.g., Romans 6:23) it is clear that "death" here means the death of the soul as well as of the body, and we believe that the same applies to the Old Testament passages. God created man such that he could have had immortality if he had obeyed Him, but he sinned and forfeited the gift, which can only be regained through the redemption that is in Christ. God did not make man to die, it is man's own fault that he is not immortal.

Some would answer that the doctrine of the Fall is an exploded myth, "which no thinking person believes in these days", and that sin is simply the victory of man's inherited beast instincts over the higher nature which evolution has produced. We reply that anyone who takes this position is most inconsistent in objecting to conditional immortality. According to this position, God did not give man the clean sheet which the Bible says He did, but allowed him to start his career with the inheritance of animal instincts from the beasts against which a slowly evolving higher nature must constantly struggle. If he can believe this of God, it is more than strange that he should insist that God gave man an immortal soul, and that without even making the immortality conditional on man's submission to Himself.

Morever, immortality without victory over sin would be a curse rather than a blessing. Even apart from the Bible teaching on the subject, it surely stands to reason that a soul which could not die but persisted in preferring evil to good would be eternally evil and eternally miserable. And in any case, if people believe in God and a future life, they must acknowledge the truth on which we have insisted in the last chapter, that man's life, whether in this world or the next, comes from God. If that be so, God surely has every right to withdraw the gift if it be misused, especially as He has provided a way of atonement, so that the barrier between man and Himself may be removed, and He is also ready to give grace to enable those who come to Him to obey His holy will.

But to some people the thought that God could so finally reject any of His creatures as to bring their existence to an end, is intolerable. "All men are His children, however disobedient and ungrateful some of them may be. Surely His love will go on striving for them in the next world as in this, until at last He wins them to Himself". It is an axiom with many people that our Lord represents God as the Father of all men. But let them get a good concordance, and study the word "father" in the Gospels. They will find that our Lord does not use the relation of father to son to illustrate God's relation to those who persist in rejecting Him. Every place where He uses the words "your Father" will be found to be in a context where He is addressing disciples. In the explanation of the Parable of the Tares, He says, "The Son of man shall send forth His angels, and they shall gather out of His kingdom all things that cause stumbling, and them that do iniquity, and shall cast them into the furnace of fire: there shall be weeping and gnashing of teeth. Then shall the righteous shine forth as the sun in the kingdom of their Father" (Matthew 13:41-43). There is no word of the Father-relationship when He is speaking of the doom of the lost, but immediately He speaks of "the righteous" He refers to their Father.

The Parable of the Prodigal Son is no exception, for its point is to represent the joy with which the Father receives the repentance of a bad son, not His relation to a son who continues hostile to Him. When the sinner comes to God in repentance, he finds Him a Father indeed, who receives him as a long-lost son. But there is nothing here or elsewhere to indicate that God regards as His children those who persist in rejecting His love. They are rather compared to disobedient or unfaithful servants, to ungrateful guests who reject a generous invitation (Matthew 22:1-7; Luke 14:16-24), to rebels against their King (Luke 19:14, 27), but not to disobedient sons.[16] We emphasize the teaching of our Lord here, because those who think that God is the Father, even of those who persist in rejecting Him, think that in this matter they are following Jesus Christ, but a careful study of His words shows that such is not the case.

The argument that surely God's patience must be limitless, and that He would never finally give up any man, sounds attractive, but the evidence already given in the earlier chapters of this book shows plainly that it does not square with the recorded teaching of Jesus Christ. This is a remarkable fact, which should give pause even to those who do not accept the authority of the Bible as final. The Gospels are the only authority which we possess as to what our Lord taught, and in no part of them is there any statement indicating that in the next world God's patience continues to bear with those who have rejected Him, and that He still seeks to win them, but there is much to indicate the contrary. Is it likely, apart from any theory of inspiration, that those who reported our Lord's sayings should have consistently misrepresented Him in this matter? If He really was wont to say that God's patience seeks the lost in the next life as in this, surely some evidence of it would survive in the records. But in fact, though the Lord Jesus gave the highest proof of His love for men which could be given, His testimony is unvarying that for those who reject His love, or falsely profess to accept it, there is only judgment in the world to come, and the door of opportunity is closed.

But even those who most fully accept our Lord's authority may recognize that there is a difficulty here which needs consideration. The difficulty is indeed increased for those who believe that even in this life God sometimes sentences a rejecter of His love to go his own way, and that He then withdraws His Spirit from pleading with

---

[16] In the Parable of the Two Sons (Matthew 21:28-31), the point is not the relationship of the sons, but what constitutes obedience, whether it is the profession of it or the act. The Father gives a command, and then takes no further part in the story.

him. Yet there are instances of human beings whose love has striven to win the ungrateful and unworthy right to the edge of the grace, persisting in the face of endless rebuffs, and sometimes without any evidence of final success. Is the love of God less persevering than that of some of His creatures?[17] Our Lord Himself told His disciples to forgive unto seventy times seven, and said, "If thy brother sin against thee seven times in a day, and seven times turn again to thee, saying I repent, thou shalt forgive him" (Luke 17:4). Why then does He Himself say that He will shut the door on those who did not enter during the appointed time, and that He will say to them, "I know not whence ye are; depart from me all ye workers of iniquity" (Luke 13:24-27)?

This difficulty arises from comparing two unlike things, the relation of man with man, and that of God with man. The differences are of vital importance.

1. The Christian to whom our Lord addresses His tremendous command to forgive without limit is himself a sinner who has been forgiven the infinite sum of his sin against God. In relation to him, the love of God has known no limit, and the Lord tells him that he must forgive his fellow-sinner without limit. God, however, is the holy Creator and King of the man who offends against Him.

2. God is not a "magnified private individual", He is the origin as well as the upholder of the eternal law of righteousness, by which is not meant a kind of enormous code, but the essential principles of justice, holiness and love. Now it is well understood that even a human being, if his relation to an offender is that of judge, or if in some other way he is responsible for upholding the law in the interests of the community, is not entitled to forgive without limit. He must punish, and in case of obstinate refusal to reform, his punishments must become more and more severe. In certain

---

[17] Dr. W.E. Maltby in *The Meaning of the Cross* gives some remarkable examples, and draws the conclusion against which we are contending here.

extreme cases he is bound to pronounce sentence of death, although the life which he takes away was not given by him. How much more is it intelligible that God, the Giver of life, should inflict the death penalty on one who has disobeyed His laws, and rejected His offer of mercy?

3. Man cannot read the heart of his fellow-man, or know the future. He is bound to hope against hope that reform is possible, even in cases which seem most unpromising, for in fact the grace of God has redeemed the most seemingly hopeless people. God, however, knows the innermost thoughts of men, and the future is as plain to Him as the present. He can make no mistakes. When he pronounces the death sentence, He is not condemning one whom more patience on His part might have saved.

Lastly, there is a similar difficulty, arising out of human analogy, which at first sight seems very formidable. If God had to give up a human soul, and sentence it to death, would it not be a defeat for Him? When a headmaster expels a boy from school, the tragedy is in a certain sense a defeat for the headmaster, and for the school system for which he is responsible: just as every execution of a criminal is a defeat of society's plans for dealing with criminals. Are we then to say that every case of the death penalty pronounced by God upon a human soul would be a defeat for Him? If so, as it is unthinkable that He should suffer defeat in any sphere, it would seem to follow that it is unthinkable that He should finally give up any soul which He has made.

Now we agree of course that God can never suffer defeat in the sense of being overpowered by something or someone stronger than Himself. We agree also that God does desire the salvation of every human soul: the New Testament expressly says so (1 Timothy 2:4). Yet we believe that, alas, many souls are not saved. But we answer that those who believe in free will in any real sense must admit the possibility of what our Lord said about the Pharisees and the lawyers, that they "rejected for themselves the counsel of God, being not baptized of him (John)" (Luke 7:30). The word here translated "counsel" never means "advice", but "will", "purpose": see, for example, Acts 2:23; 13:36; Ephesians 1:11. God's provisional will for those Pharisees, that which His love would have had them do, was that they should accept the baptism of John, and thereby be prepared to accept the Lord Jesus. They rejected, or made of no effect, that loving desire of His, to their own ruin. So also the desire of God, in a certain sense, for all men is that they should be saved, but many reject His loving will for them, and perish, not because they are stronger than He, but because He does not use His power to coerce their wills.

In sum, our answer to the objection is that it is true that every time a human soul perishes, it means that that soul has refused to accept God's purpose of love to save it, as our Lord said of the Pharisees. But this is not rightly termed a defeat for God, because His power has not attempted to compel them to salvation against their wills.[18]

It may be answered that this is an evasion, because in the human analogy no one expects a headmaster to coerce his boys' wills, in a supernatural sense, and yet if he feels compelled to expel a boy, he is acknowledging a defeat. Here, as always when man is compared with God, the comparison is only partially true. If that schoolmaster knew that he possessed perfect wisdom and a perfect knowledge of the boy's character, and that he had made no mistakes in dealing with him, or in organizing his school system, he would be entitled to deny that he had suffered any defeat: for nothing could have prevented the tragedy, except the coercion of the boy's will, which would have been undesirable even had it been possible. Actually however, he knows very well that he is not omniscient or perfect, and that though he may have done his best, more might possibly have been done had he possessed the necessary knowledge and

---

[18] Of course this is only one side of the truth. There is an eternal "counsel" of God, which no man can ever reject or frustrate with regard to himself: for God is sovereign, and not only does He know what will be, but also nothing happens which is not in a certain sense in His plan. This is the dark mystery of Predestination, which is equally true with the fact of free will. But the discussion of that problem is outside the scope of the present book.

personal gifts. For this reason, if he is a conscientious and sensitive man, he cannot escape a sense of defeat. Thus the analogy fails.

We have been considering in this chapter two main objections to the idea that any human soul could perish. The first is based on considerations concerned with man. Some object to conditional immortality and, in effect, state that it is contrary to the essential implications of Christianity regarding the worth of human personality, and also to a deep instinct of human nature, which on Christian principles, must be God-given. We have shown that the objection misconceives the true Christian position as regards man in rebellion against God, and that the argument from instinct has force only as an evidence for survival of bodily death, which is not the question. And we have contended that God did not make man for death, it was by his own sin that he forfeited immortality.

The second main objection is concerned with the character of God. It is argued that it is unthinkable that God should finally reject any of His human creatures. This objection rests partly on the belief that He is the Father of all men, whatever their attitude to Him may be: we gave briefly the reasons, which we have set out more fully elsewhere,[19] for concluding that this belief does not accord with our Lord's teaching. But the objection also rests on human analogies. It is contended that human beings have been known to show a patience with the ungrateful and unresponsive which endured to the end of earthly life. Surely then God, whose love is infinite and perfect, will continue even beyond this present world His efforts to win the rebellious to Himself. And it is asked whether a sentence of death passed on a human soul would not be a defeat for God, even as in a sense a death sentence on earth is a defeat for the efforts of society to deal with criminals. We have shown that the seeming strength of these objections arises from ignoring the essential difference between the relations of man with men and those of God with men.

The teaching of the Lord Jesus Christ on the finality of God's judgments is plain and uncompromising, and no one knows God

---

[19] *Why the Cross?* Chapter 2.

better than He, nor has anyone given a greater proof of love for men than He has given. Assaults upon His representation of God's judgments may be plausible, but they must fail, and they do fail.

Chapter 12: Objections to Penal Suffering

"The Son of Man shall send forth His angels . . . the angels shall come forth, and sever the wicked from among the righteous, and shall cast them into the furnace of fire: there shall be the weeping and gnashing of teeth" (Matthew 13:41, 49, 50). These and similar words raise the most formidable of all the difficulties connected with this awful subject. If it be granted that God might pass sentence of final death on those who reject Him, how could it be thought that He would sentence them to die by the torment of fire? Let it not be thought for one moment that acceptance of the Bible teaching about Hell means indifference to these difficulties. We who believe without reserve in the truth of our Lord's words of judgment tremble as we read them, all the more because we do believe. But we know that He who spoke those words is Love and Truth, and we are sure that He would never have said them unless they were true.

But part of the difficulty probably arises from a too literal and material understanding of Bible symbols. The present writer would not dare to say dogmatically that there is not a physical element in the suffering of hell: we do not know enough to be dogmatic about these things. But surely it is highly probable that "fire" is symbolic of some kind of spiritual suffering. It is hard to understand how the devil and his demon servants could suffer physically. We must not indeed imagine that the sufferings are less dreadful for being spiritual. Even in this life some of us know how awful agony of mind can be. And whatever the sufferings of hell are, our Lord has chosen the torment of fire, perhaps the most dreadful of physical sufferings, to be the symbol of them. But though spiritual sufferings would not be less awful than physical torments, yet, if the sufferings are spiritual, it is possible that they may be the inevitable result of the sinner's own sin, working upon the soul from within, rather than a torment inflicted upon it from without. Of course external circumstances would play their part, and hell would be the "furnace of fire" because of the awful conditions, beyond our imagining, of an existence without God in the companionship of demons and wicket men. Even if there is a kind of physical element in the sufferings, for we do not forget that soul *and body* (the resurrection body) are destroyed in hell, it may be that the physical sufferings are caused rather by the reaction of mind on body than by physical torments inflicted upon the body from without.

So far we have not ventured to say more than "it is possible", or "it may be", for any opinions on this subject must be advanced with the utmost caution. But the suggestions offered above seem to be possible in themselves, and are not in conflict with the imagery used in the Bible. The judgment is still the judgment of God, but the connection between sin and its punishment is far more direct and immediate than if we think of torment inflicted from without.

Moreover this way of understanding the sufferings of hell helps us to meet a tremendous difficulty, which can be put in this form. On earth *torment implies a tormentor*, a dreadful being who inflicts suffering, and is morally destroyed in so doing. Who then is the tormentor of the souls in hell? In past generations men have actually said that God "upholds the lost with one hand, and torments them with the other": others, who have shrunk from so hideous a conception, have supposed that the lost are tormented by the demons, their companions in misery. The Bible says nothing whatever in support of notions such as these. We have suggested that the sufferings of hell may be mainly from within, the outworking of the sin which has finally cut off the soul from God, and torments it till it brings it to its miserable end.

But even if in truth the suffering is more external than we have supposed, one thing is clear: it is the inevitable result of being in hell, it does not consist of torments devised for the souls in hell by God, as Dante imagined. The last judgment of God condemns those who have rejected Him to the "furnace of fire", the eternal fire prepared for the devil and his angels", the "lake of fire, which is the second death". To be there means inevitably to suffer. But there is no question of a tormentor.

But still, whatever may be said, the mind shudders at, and shrinks back from the thought of human beings suffering torments in hell, even though the torments may be mainly or entirely spiritual, and though we do not believe that they will be everlasting. Now we have often called attention to the fact that these terrible sayings about the fire of hell come mainly from the words of the Lord Jesus Christ, the Friend of sinners, who gave His life for them upon the Cross. And He speaks of Himself as the Judge who will pronounce these awful judgments. How is this fact to be explained? The only possible explanation is that He perfectly understood and shared His Father's abhorrence of sin; that He, being God, saw sin as God sees it.[20]

If we could fully understand what sin means to God, we should understand His judgment of it, even the awful judgment of the lake of fire. There is one thing, other than the lake of fire, whereby God's opposition to sin can be measured, and that is the Cross of Christ. The greatest proof of His love for man is at the same time the greatest evidence of His condemnation of sin. The Divine Son of God emptied Himself of His glory, and took man's nature upon Him, so that He might become our Sin-Bearer. Then it is written that "Jehovah laid on Him the iniquity of us all", "Him who knew no sin He made to be sin on our behalf, that we might become the righteousness of God through Him" (Isaiah 53:6; 2 Corinthians 5:21). Our Divine Saviour suffered not only awful physical agony on the cross, "but also the unspeakable spiritual horror of becoming identified with the sin to which He was infinitely opposed, and thereby coming under the curse of sin".[21] That cry of uttermost anguish, "My God, my God, why hast Thou forsaken Me?" gives us some idea of what it cost God to forgive sin. The fact that He should be willing to pay so awful a price for our redemption, rather

---

[20] It is important to observe that God's opposition is to the sin in the first instance, not to the sinner. He loves the sinner and has provided a way whereby he may be separated from his sin and become acceptable to Him. If however he refuses to be separated from it, he must perish in the judgment which God must visit upon his sin. See sections 'General Remarks on the Doctrine' and 'The Awfulness of the Second Death' in chapter 8.

[21] *Why the Cross?* p. 186.

than simply forgive their sin without cost, as some would have had Him do, reveals how tremendous is His opposition to sin. But the measure is itself immeasurable. We cannot fully grasp what the Atonement cost God, because our minds are limited: but in so far as we can understand Calvary, in so far we can see what sin means to God.

Here then is the fundamental answer to the problem of the severity of God's judgments. Sin nailed His Son to the Cross. If men prefer sin to God, then that awful opposition to sin which made Calvary necessary must fall upon them, and we have no right to complain that His justice is not satisfied with the infliction of a painless death.

But we shall obtain further light on this problem is we consider certain special difficulties connected with the doctrine of Conditional Immortality. If the ultimate sentence on the condemned is always the extinction of existence, why is it not inflicted on them at the time of bodily death? Why should they suffer a "resurrection of judgment" (John 5:29), in order that they may be condemned to perish in hell? From one point of view we have already answered this objection, by showing that it arises from a defective sense of the blackness of sin in God's sight. But this is an answer which fails to convince some people.

For the defender of the latter doctrine can say, "Because the soul cannot die, those who reject God must, by the necessities of the case, spend all eternity without God, and for that reason alone they must be eternally miserable. And further, those who are not with God can be nowhere else than with His enemy, the devil, in the eternal fire prepared for him". In other words, given the two premises of the immortality of every soul and the impossibility of repentance after death, everlasting misery is the only possible fate for the man who rejects God in this life.

Of course it is possible to reply to this argument that God, if He willed, could ordain things differently, so that His creatures should not be subjected to so awful a fate: and we, for our part, believe that He has ordained things differently. Still, superficially at least, the defender of the traditional doctrine might seem to have an easier task in this respect than we have, who acknowledge that the ultimate fate of the wicked is the end of conscious existence, and must answer the question, "Then why torment them first?" In earthly justice, it is acknowledged by all civilized people that the death penalty is the supreme punishment, and that no unnecessary suffering should ever be added to it, no matter how great the wickedness of the criminal may have been. Shall God be less merciful than men? The sinner dies, why not let him remain dead, body and soul as well, why raise him up to a resurrection of judgment, in order that he may suffer a terrible penalty before his existence is finally ended? This suffering cannot do him any good, for it is to end in death: it is merely vindictive, and therefore merely cruel.

Here we must remember what we have so often pointed out before, that neither the rights nor the responsibilities of the human administrator of justice can be compared with those of God. Let there be no misunderstanding. We are not contending that because God is Almighty and man is His creature, therefore He can do what He likes, and is not subject to the restrictions which affect men in relation to one another: though there is a sense in which this is true. God is Almighty of course, but He is also perfectly holy and we have no wish to plead a defence which might seem to amount to "Might is Right". The case is quite otherwise.

The responsibilities of the human judge are limited. He is not concerned to vindicate the eternal laws of righteousness, but to protect the community from the criminal. His rights are also limited. He is not the giver of life, and if the supreme necessity of safeguarding the community forces him to take away the criminal's life, he has gone to the furthest limit of his rights over a fellow creature. Needless suffering inflicted on the criminal in the execution of the death penalty could do no good to anyone, and would be mere cruelty. If two murderers come before a judge, one of whom has quickly killed his victim in a fit of passion, while the other has put his victim to death with revolting cruelty, gloating over his sufferings, the human judge has no right to pass any severer sentence on the second murderer than the quick death which he ordains the first. Society must be protected from them both, the criminal world must know that death is the penalty for murder,[22] that others may fear to do likewise, but the human judge has neither the right to go further than this, nor the responsibility for redressing the balance of desert between the two men. He is not their Maker. He can only send them to face their trial before One Who can and will do what he neither can do, nor ought to attempt to do. Again and again human justice is forced to acknowledge its powerlessness to deal with human sin on the basis of its deserts, because that is not its function. The judge is not dealing with *sin* which is an outrage against God and His eternal laws, but with *crime*, which is an offence against the community of fellow-creatures and fellow-sinners.

If the penalty for the vilest wickedness were a painless extinction of existence, many of the worst inequalities of earth would go eternally unredressed. A blackmailer grows rich by inflicting on his victims agonies of mind equal to the most dreadful physical tortures: he contrives to escape human justice, and he goes to the grave rich and prosperous. Some of his victims have lived and died without God, and cannot therefore receive the gift of eternal life. Are all alike merely to perish at death, as do the beasts? Will the justice of God have nothing to say to that scoundrel, but the same judgment which He has for his unhappy victims, whose cries of anguish have continually come up to Him? Many of the victims of the Nazi concentration camps may have rejected Jesus Christ, and refused to own Him as Lord: alas, they must "perish", unless the all-wise Judge deems that their opportunity has not been sufficient. But will God make no difference between them and the brutal guards who tormented them, and the still worse brutes who taught those guards to enjoy and admire cruelty?

The Christian is forbidden to revenge himself, and is commanded to pray for his persecutor, that his heart may be turned while there is time. But the basis of this command is, "Vengeance is Mine, I

---

[22] This book was, of course, written before the present legislation on capital punishment.

will repay, saith the Lord" (Romans 12:19 A.V.).[23] We are living in days when the awful possibilities of human wickedness are being revealed, as they have not been for centuries, and faith would have a hard task indeed, if it could not be sure that God will demand a full account for all the abominable cruelties and wrongs that are done on earth. And this would be impossible, if the only alternative to eternal life were a painless end to existence at the time of bodily death. The resurrection to judgment, and the infliction of penal suffering, are absolutely essential to the justice of God.

But it would not be a fair argument to mention only very extreme cases, such as the blackmailer and the torturer, in order to win assent for a doctrine which goes much further than such instances as those. No theory of future punishment which does not provide for such extremes of wickedness can be true, yet they are not the only cases to be considered. In the New Testament, the fire of hell is spoken of as the penalty for sins which, in our eyes at least, are much less dark than blackmail or torture. He who would cling to anything, however dear, which might "cause him to stumble", (i.e., cause him to offend against God) is warned of the danger in hell fire, so too is he who forgets God, and is indifferent to his neighbour's need, because he is absorbed in the acquisition and enjoyment of earthly wealth. Weeping and gnashing of teeth are included in the doom of those who profess to belong to the Church of Christ, when in reality they are sons of the evil one (Matthew 13:38, 41, 49, 50); who profess to be His servants but misuse their position as such (Matthew 24:48-51), or even fail to use the gifts committed to them for God's service (Matthew 25:14-30). They too who have been in contact with the Lord through His Gospel, and yet have neglected to go in through the narrow door of opportunity while it still remained open, are warned that they will weep and gnash their teeth when they see the patriarchs and prophets in the kingdom of God, and themselves cast forth without

---

[23] This does not mean that the Christian should rejoice, from the standpoint of personal satisfaction, in the vengeance of God on even the worst of men. But it does mean that he assents to His justice, which will not allow such actions to go unpunished, and indeed would not be perfect if it did.

(Luke 23:24-28). For these sins, as well as for wronging the young and innocent, or deliberately inflicting dreadful suffering on their fellow men, God has ordained that there shall be retributive suffering, as part of the doom of eternal death.

But we must remember two things. First, all sin is sin against God: and offences which are directly and immediately against Him are certainly not treated as of small account by Him, merely because no obvious injury has been done to the sinner's fellow-men. He is man's Creator, and He has offered him a wonderful salvation, for which His own Son offered Himself on the Cross, and suffered agony unthinkable of mind and body. If this priceless gift be scorned, and the Creator and Redeemer treated as of no account throughout a man's life, or if gifts of personal influence, which might have been used in God's service, are used instead to turn others away from Him, the sinner is not going to slip into oblivion at death, but he will share to some degree, proportioned to his guilt in God's sight, in the awful punishment of the devil whom he has served instead of God. That this should be so is terrible, but it is also just.

Again, he who has professed obedience to God, but has made the outward membership of His Church a cloak for wickedness, will come under a dreadful punishment, not only for what he may have done to his fellow-men, but for the insult to the Blood of Christ by which he professed to have been redeemed. This too is just, however terrible.

Secondly, the fact of gradation of punishment, which would be impossible if there were no penal suffering, gives room for a perfect administration of justice. God, the all-wise reader of hearts, knows exactly the degrees of each man's sin and of his responsibility for it, and He judges according to His infinite wisdom, and makes no mistakes.

It may seem at first sight, hard to understand how a just and holy God can raise sinners from the dead in order to punish them in hell before they finally perish, yet a closer examination of the matter makes plain that so only could there be a righteous administration of justice, and a final redressing of the inequalities of this world.

Chapter 13: General Conclusion

In this book we have not been faced with the terrible task of defending the traditional doctrine of everlasting torment. Though the doctrine which we believe to be Scriptural is not free from very real and important difficulties, we trust that the foregoing pages have shown that it can be reconciled with belief in the Love of God without imposing an unbearable strain on the mind and conscience of the believer.

In the last three chapters we have been examining the difficulties of the Scriptural doctrine, and we have found that they have their origin either in a misunderstanding of the Christian position, or in attempts to use analogies, drawn from the relations of men to one another, which are inapplicable to the essentially different relations of God to man, or in a defective sense of the awfulness of sin in God's sight.

We are all naturally inclined to fall into the latter two classes of fallacy. We cannot fully understand God, and we inevitably tend to reason from the human, of which we know much, to the Divine, of which we know little. And the best of us knows so imperfectly what sin is to God that we find the awful severity of His judgments very hard to understand. But it is just because we are deficient in these respects, that God has given us His word to tell us, from Himself, what the truth of these matters it. It is then natural and only to be expected, that we should find the teaching of the Bible about God's judgments difficult. But a recognition of the causes of our difficulties should drive us back to a humble acceptance of what God has revealed.

And if we turn from these objections to consider the positive reasons for accepting the explanation of eternal punishment, which we have shown to be in accordance with the Word of God, we shall find that (in the words of some with whom the present writer has discussed it) this explanation "makes sense". The awfulness of sin in God's sight is fully recognized, as it must be in any doctrine which is true to the Word of God, and there is nothing in the doctrine which in anyway diminishes the tremendous urgency of the appeal to the sinner to accept salvation *now*. Yet on the other hand, we are not asked to believe that God sentences any of His creatures to be tormented to all eternity, and we can look forward, with Paul, to a future when God shall be all in all, and evil shall not only be conquered but shall have ceased to exist.

More on this subject

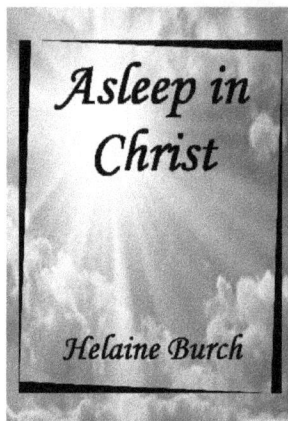

The Destiny of the Damned

Arnold V Page

Hell and Judgement In the Book of Revelation

Colin Sweet

Sheol & Hades

Their Meaning and Usage in the Word of God.

E W Bullinger

Asleep in Christ

Helaine Burch

Details of the books above, and those on the next page, can be seen on **www.obt.org.uk**

They can be ordered from that website.

They are also available as eBooks from Amazon and Apple, and as paperbacks from Amazon.

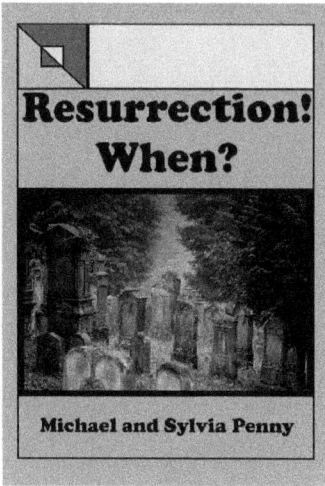

Resurrection! When?

Michael and Sylvia Penny

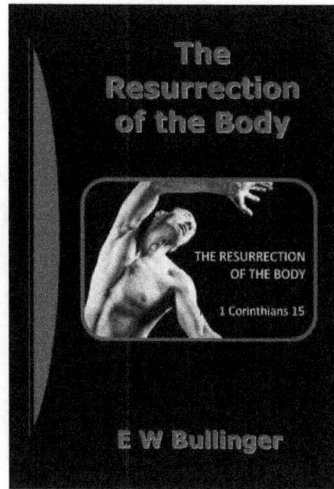

The Resurrection of the Body

THE RESURRECTION OF THE BODY

1 Corinthians 15

E W Bullinger

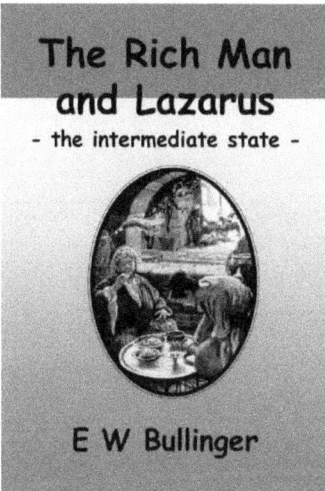

The Rich Man and Lazarus
- the intermediate state -

E W Bullinger

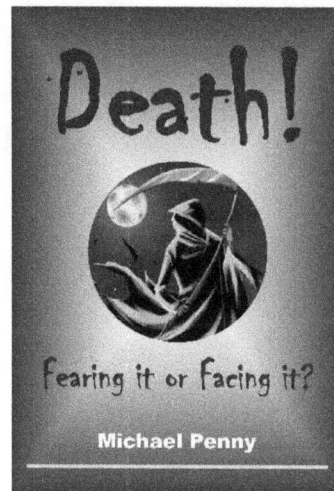

Death!

fearing it or facing it?

Michael Penny

Publications of The Open Bible Trust must be in accordance with its evangelical, fundamental and dispensational basis. However, beyond this minimum, writers are free to express whatever beliefs they may have as their own understanding, provided that the aim in so doing is to further the object of The Open Bible Trust. A copy of the doctrinal basis is available on **www.obt.org.uk or** from:

THE OPEN BIBLE TRUST
Fordland Mount, Upper Basildon,
Reading, RG8 8LU, UK

www.ingramcontent.com/pod-product-compliance
Lightning Source LLC
Chambersburg PA
CBHW061754020426
42331CB00006B/1482